Lana

THE LIFE AND LOVES OF LANA TURNER

* *Jane Ellen Wayne* *

ST. MARTIN'S PRESS
NEW YORK

Design by Sara Stemen

ISBN: 0-312-11356-0

First Edition: March 1995
10 9 8 7 6 5 4 3 2 1

To the Survivor

✳ CONTENTS ✳

$\mathcal{S}$HE WAS WEARING A CLINGING WOOL sweater, tight skirt, spiked heels, and a saucy beret. As she walked down the street, her ample bosom moved to the rhythm of "Dixie" being played by a band in the Memorial Day parade. The young girl's bouncing breasts were subtle enough to pass Hollywood censors in 1937 but tantalizing enough to arouse every male in the audience. To the men's disappointment, she's not seen again because her character in the movie is raped and killed, but not before the screen had given birth to a legend.

She was called the Sweater Girl, and the label stuck. What a coincidence because *Lana*, translated into Spanish, means "wool." She was only seventeen, but she wanted her name pronounced *Lana*, as in *lah-de-dah*, thank you.

She got her first speaking part in *They Won't Forget* (and they didn't!) because Lana was "dimpled, innocent and sexy," a rare combination. She retained that natural, breathless little-girl quality in her voice, which blended ideally with a youthful face that somehow defied aging. When Lana became a blonde, she took on the sophistication of a well-bred but innocent debutante.

Louis B. Mayer, head of Metro-Goldwyn-Mayer, preferred the all-American type with a clean image. Lana was one of his favorite contract players despite her many love affairs, abortions, divorces, and scandals. MGM was the best finishing school in the world, but there were no graduates. Only beautiful and pampered famous movie icons who were eventually stranded without Papa Mayer.

When Lana left MGM after eighteen years, she remained true to the studio system, never leaving home without looking her best. Forever the star. Not a hair out of place or a dark root showing. Her makeup was perfect, her fingernails beautifully manicured and her clothes neatly pressed.

A few years ago a fire broke out in Lana's apartment building. Forced to evacuate, she grabbed three items: her cigarettes, her lipstick, and her hairdryer. That, my friends, is a movie star of the Golden Era.

Chapter 1

✳ THE IMAGE ✳

𝓕OLLOWING A BITTER PARTING FROM LANA, her secretary and companion, Taylor Pero, wrote a book in 1982 about their ten years together. Not so coincidentally did Lana come out with her autobiography, *The Lady, the Legend, the Truth,* the same year. Pero did not strip Lana of her glorious image by relating his story. Unfortunately, she clung to her throne and came across as a virgin queen. In her defense, she knew no other way to tell her life's story. Lana wrote that she'd never cared much for sex. Why had she volunteered this information when every red-blooded man in the world thought she did? Her strict MGM upbringing was partly to blame. Lana counterattacked Taylor Pero's exposé by giving the public some new juicy tidbits about herself and then closed the door in the readers' faces.

Almost ten years later Mickey Rooney wrote about his escapades with Lana when they attended MGM's "little red schoolhouse." She came out of hibernation and denied it on "Entertainment Tonight." Mickey's only comment was "Well, if it didn't happen, it was the best damn dream I ever had!" In his prime Mickey had no problem getting women. He was number one at the box office when Lana dated him, not to mention his wealth and dynamic energy.

If Ava Gardner married Mickey for love, he had to be a special guy. But fifty years later, Lana went out of her way to deny she gave in to Rooney's advances. Silly, but then she claimed to be a virgin until the age of nineteen, and it was a distinguished attorney who was her first lover. That's more romantic than smooching with Mickey in the backseat of his convertible.

Despite Lana's long list of lovers, she was a romantic at heart. Moonlight and roses and diamond rings. She liked to live in style but was not particularly interested in rich men. There had to be chemistry and lots of it. If Lana took notice of a man and straightened her shoulders, it was only a matter of time before he was lured in her direction. Lana loved to flirt regardless of her intentions. This was part of her charming allure and sometimes her downfall. Seven marriages within a span of twenty-nine years, for example. Yet the man she wanted above all others got away.

Lana married someone else on the rebound, turned to pills and alcohol, and attempted suicide. Her fourth husband physically abused her daughter, Cheryl, but this could not compare with the teenager's involvement in the death of her mother's gangster lover in 1958. There are those who still think Lana had some responsibility. Others have speculated that the handsome hood was having an affair with both mother and daughter. All this remains nothing more than conjecture, for it appears that Cheryl came to Lana's defense during a life-threatening argument, and, in the confusion, the burly gangster sealed his own fate.

Walter Winchell, the most powerful newspaper columnist in the world, came to Lana's defense during the inquest: "She is made of rays of sun, woven of blue eyes, honey-colored hair and flowing curves. She is Lana Turner, goddess of the screen. But soon the magician leaves and the shadows take over. She is lashed by vicious report-

ing. . . . Give your heart to the girl with the broken
heart. . . ."

Actress Gloria Swanson retorted, "Walter, I think it is
disgusting that you are trying to whitewash Lana. She is
not even an actress . . . she is only a trollop!"

The verdict was "justifiable homicide," but Lana lived
in fear of the gangster's mob boss, who did not agree with
the jury. That Cheryl's father was given custody of her
prompted the press to label Lana an unfit mother. Word
got around Hollywood that Lana Turner's career was over.
Instead, she made a remake of *Imitation of Life*, a title that
some critics thought quite appropriate. Lana had to be
coaxed into doing the movie for fear of being blackballed
and tackling a role that required more than a pretty face.
But the film was a big success, and Lana laughed all the
way to the bank with 50 percent of the profits.

Lana married three more times—to two businessmen
and a then hypnotist, whom she divorced in 1972. Taylor
Pero was her secretary at the time and became her constant
companion. Though Lana was something of a recluse, she
did a weekly television show and appeared on the stage.
She retired in 1983.

Her daughter, Cheryl, went through hard times, trying to put the shattered pieces of her own life together.
But like her mother, she is a survivor. Cheryl lives with
her beautiful lover, Joyce "Josh" LeRoy, who shared the
bad and good times with the bewildered child of a movie
goddess. If Lana was shocked to find out Cheryl was a
lesbian, she soon realized her daughter had found lasting
happiness and the three are very close.

As of this writing, Lana Turner has inoperable throat
cancer that has spread to her neck and jaw, but friends say
she's in good "spirits." A hairdresser comes to her twelve-
room apartment twice a week. Lana gets regular facials and

massages, though she only ventures out for radiation treatments.

Before Lana became ill, she turned down many offers to appear on television. "I don't need the money," she said, "and I don't want people looking at me, saying, 'Gosh, she's old.' I want my fans to remember me as I was."

There's so much to be remembered about Lana aside from her beauty. She's lived such a full life it overflows with tears of joy and laughter.

Chapter 2

✳ THE EARLY YEARS ✳

*T*HE CUTE WELL-ROUNDED YOUNG LADY whose breasts bounced to the tune of "Dixie" was born Julia Jean Turner in Wallace, Idaho, a small mining town, on February 8, 1921. She was a true American hybrid, with a mixture of Scotch, Irish, Dutch and English ancestry. Her mother, Mildred Frances Cowan, came from Arkansas; her father, John Virgil, a miner, was from Alabama and spoke with a thick Southern accent. They'd met at a dance in Picher, Oklahoma. She was fifteen and traveling with her father, who disapproved of the relationship. But Virgil would not be put off. He was twenty-four years old and knew what he wanted. Mildred eloped with him to Wallace, Idaho, and a year later Julia ("Judy") was born. Virgil worked in the mines, but he probably made as much money gambling. He was an excellent cardplayer, but the odds were not always in his favor. The Turners traveled from town to town and settled wherever Virgil could find work. He was a happy-go-lucky guy who preferred making a living at bootlegging or at the poker table, with or without a dime. Virgil would come home in the evening, play the Victrola, and dance around the living room with his wife and little Judy.

Lana later said that she took after her father, having inherited his small nose, blue eyes, and devil-make-care attitude. To hell with the consequences.

Mildred was very much in love with the man she referred to as "Mr. Turner," but she was hardly prepared for the duties of wife and mother at the age of sixteen. Her wedding night was so traumatic that she came to hate and avoid sex, but Virgil had his way with her. Mildred's second pregnancy resulted in a miscarriage.

In 1927 the Turners drove to San Francisco, where Virgil predicted new beginnings. Once again he looked for a regular job but returned to a life of bootlegging and gambling. After he was arrested and fined, Mildred decided they should separate. She found work as a hairdresser and Judy went to live with friends, whom she later referred to as "foster parents." To pay for bed and board Judy shared household chores—cleaning, cooking, washing, and ironing. Two years later Mildred noticed bruises and cuts on Judy's body where she had been whipped with a stick. Desperate, Mildred reconciled with Virgil, but living conditions were worse than ever. Drinking and gambling, he would disappear for days, forcing Mildred to go begging for food and lodging.

Judy made friends, went to the movies, and regularly attended services at the Catholic church, even though she had been baptized a Protestant. Mildred gave her permission to convert, and at her christening she chose the names of saints Mildred and Frances, after her mother. (Lana's given name is often listed as Julia Jean Mildred Frances Turner.) When Virgil found out about his daughter's conversion he was furious but unable to do anything about it. Lana said in later years that she knew little about religion at that time. It was the colorful pageantry that drew her to the Catholic Church.

On December 14, 1930, Virgil was robbed, beaten, and killed after winning big at a crap game. His body was found on the street with one sock missing—the sock in which he stashed his money. Lana recalled, "The shock I suffered then may be a valid excuse for me now. It may explain things I myself do not understand."

Mildred and Judy shared a friend's apartment and were grateful for whatever they had at the height of the Depression. By 1935 the Turner women were living a fairly normal life, until a persistent cough began taking its toll on Mildred. When a doctor suggested a drier climate in Southern California, Mildred called her friend Gladys Taylor in Los Angeles. "Stay with me," Gladys said. "I have plenty of room."

Judy was fifteen when she and her mother moved to Los Angeles. Lana said that getting into the movies was not their motive. If anything, she wanted to be a dress designer. Mildred somehow managed to have nice clothes, and she saw to it that her daughter did also. Judy said, "If I ever make a lot of money, I'll make sure that my mother has a beautiful wardrobe." She kept her promise.

After only a month at Hollywood High School Judy decided to cut class and have a Coke at the Top Hat Café across the street. As she was sipping her soda Judy noticed a man, who was sitting across the counter, watching her. This well-dressed gentleman finally spoke to the manager, who came over to Judy and said, "The man over there—Mr. Wilkerson—would like to meet you. He's a friend of mine."

She nodded, and the good-looking gentleman with a mustache walked around the counter and introduced himself. He asked Judy if she wanted to be an actress. She didn't know.

"Every pretty young girl wants to be in the movies and I think you'd be perfect," he said, handing her his business card.

Judy said she'd give it to her mother.

"Have her call me," he said.

Mildred was exhausted by the time she got home from work that evening and paid little attention to Judy's story about the man in the Top Hat Café. But Gladys Turner knew right away that Billy Wilkerson published a well-known newspaper, the *Hollywood Reporter*.

Since Mildred had to work, she asked Gladys to call Wilkerson about an appointment the following day. He was honest about not being able to get Judy into the movies personally, but he knew the right people. He told her she was very pretty and that she had as good a chance as anyone else. But first she would need an agent. Wilkerson gave her an introductory letter to Zeppo Marx, who had a talent agency. He agreed to represent Judy and assigned agent Henry Willson to take her around to the studio casting directors. She earned twenty dollars as an extra in *A Star Is Born*, with Frederic March and Janet Gaynor, released in 1937. Otherwise there were no offers.

Director Mervyn LeRoy was looking for a girl to appear in *They Won't Forget*. Though it wasn't a big acting role, the whole plot revolved around the girl's unsolved murder. She had to be young and sexy, but innocent and cute at the same time. The casting director at Warner Brothers said, "If a girl is sexy, she's not innocent. You're asking me to find the impossible."

LeRoy interviewed at least fifty young girls before he saw Judy Turner in December 1936. "Her hair was dark, messy, uncombed," he remembered. "Her hands were trembling so she could hardly read the script. But she had that sexy-innocent-clean quality I wanted. A youthful face, but there was something smoldering underneath and she had a fantastic figure."

LeRoy said the only thing wrong with the girl was her name. "I liked Judy and I liked Turner, but they didn't go together. She reminded me of someone I knew many years ago. Her name was Donna. So I went down the alphabet. When I got to the Ls, that was it. Lonna. No, we'd spell it Lana. Judy liked it and her mother approved."

During the filming of *They Won't Forget*, Mervyn LeRoy realized that Lana had more appeal than he'd thought. She knew her lines, took directions well, and came across on the screen with that magic something that movie stars are made of. He signed her to a contract on February 22, 1937, for fifty dollars a week.

Lana and Mildred went to the preview of *They Won't Forget* and were shocked when "that thing" walked on the screen. As the girl swayed fore and aft, Mildred whispered, "Good lord!" and crouched down in her seat. Lana did too when she heard men in the audience whistle and howl. "We snuck out and jumped into a taxi," she said.

The bra that Lana wore in the movie was made of lined silk with no uplift, allowing her breasts to move freely. Mervyn LeRoy was a classy director who knew how far to go without being vulgar. Lana's hips were slim, but she moved them gracefully, and a tight skirt did the rest.

LeRoy also used Lana in *The Great Garrick*, a comedy with Brian Aherne and Olivia de Havilland, but the Sweater Girl was hidden in heavy costumes, hats, and wigs. It was a good experience for her nonetheless.

From the day Lana first sipped a five-cent Coke in her high-school hangout, she was guided by two of the most respected and influential men in Hollywood. Billy Wilkerson's newspaper was read by everyone in the film industry. He could make or break a potential movie star. So what was he doing in the Top Hat Café? It seems that Billy liked pretty young girls, but admiring them was the extent of this folly, apparently. Despite his first meeting with Lana, he wasn't in the habit of using the worn-out "How would you like to be in the movies?" routine. Perhaps his review of Lana in *They Won't Forget* explains what he saw in her: "Short on playing time is the role of the murdered schoolgirl. But as played by Lana Turner it is worthy of more than passing note. This young lady has vivid beauty, personality, and charm."

Mervyn LeRoy, born in 1900, directed such films as *Little Caesar* (1930) and had wanted a then-unknown Clark Gable to play the part of Joe Massara. Jack Warner saw Gable's screen test and laughed out loud. "You've just wasted five hundred bucks on that test," he told LeRoy. "Did you see the size of that guy's ears?" (Massara was a co-starring role in the film and wound up being played by Douglas Fairbanks, Jr., a role that boosted his career.)

Mervyn argued that Gable had something, but Warner refused to change his mind. When Lana came along seven years later, Mervyn was not about to make the same mistake and signed her to a contract. LeRoy is remembered for producing *The Wizard of Oz* and directing *Waterloo Bridge, Random Harvest, Little Women, Quo Vadis?*, and *Mister Roberts*. He directed Lana in *Johnny Eager* with Robert Taylor in 1941 and *Homecoming* with Clark Gable in 1948.

Sam Goldwyn borrowed Lana in 1937 for *The Adventures of Marco Polo*. Gary Cooper was the star, but she never got to see him. Lana played an Oriental handmaiden in two brief scenes with Alan Hale. Her dialogue consisted of four lines. Legend has it that Lana's eyebrows were shaved, a common practice in Hollywood. Actually, black slanted brows were glued on with fishnet and pulled off at the end of each day. By the time Lana finished the film her own brows had disappeared completely and they never grew back, forcing her to paint them on for the rest of her life.

When Lana later became famous, she was given star billing with Gary Cooper on theater marquees in *The Adventures of Marco Polo*. Unsuspecting moviegoers were disappointed to see her in only two scenes, but the gimmick sold more tickets at the box office.

Knowing Lana was incredibly naive about life, LeRoy spent a great deal of time showing her how to dress and behave in public. He bought Lana an evening gown for her first formal affair, but when he saw her in it, LeRoy regretted not having assigned a wardrobe lady to assist. The next day he spoke to Lana about the huge fake diamond ring she wore. "You're too beautiful to rely on false things," he said. "Wait awhile and you'll have real diamonds."

Lana thanked him. "No one had taken the time to explain these things to me," she said. Years later she told Mervyn, "I kept that big gaudy ring in my jewelry case with the real stuff as a reminder."

Lana's first big night out in Hollywood was the premiere of *The Life of Emile Zola* at Grauman's Chinese Theater on Hollywood Boulevard. From the limousine, she and her escort, actor Don Barry, walked on a red carpet into the theater. The studio arranged other dates, but Mildred was particularly fond of Barry because he resembled Virgil.

*   *   *

In 1938 Mervyn LeRoy accepted an offer from MGM that
he could not turn down. "Six thousand a week was a lot of
money," he said. Warner Brothers wasn't interested in
Lana, so Mervyn gave her a raise and took Lana with him
to Metro. "A hundred dollars a week was a lot of money!"
she said.

The few extra dollars made it possible for Lana and
Mildred to rent a furnished three-bedroom house in Laurel
Canyon. Lana bought an old car that got her to and from
work. It was a Willys Knight that cost fifty dollars.

LeRoy had no problem selling Lana to MGM. She signed
a contract with the most prestigious and powerful movie
studio in Hollywood on February 20, 1938. Because Lana
had not yet graduated from high school, she was forced to
attend MGM's "little red schoolhouse." The quaint one-
story building was actually white and located on the MGM
lot. Miss Macdonald was the schoolmarm who taught such
starstruck kids as Judy Garland, Jackie Cooper, and Elizabeth Taylor over the years. They were supposed to attend
classes five days a week, but the studio got around this by
having them tutored in their dressing rooms in the after-
noons.

Mickey Rooney, the same age as Lana, was mesmer-
ized by her from the outset. In his autobiography, *Life Is
Too Short*, Mickey wrote that he was pleasantly surprised
to discover that Lana was "as oversexed as I was." They
dated for a while, but then she stopped seeing him. Mickey
thought nothing about it until Lana told him a few years
later that she had aborted his baby. It was a shock to
Mickey, but he commented in his memoirs that perhaps it

was best that she never told him. "I might have wanted her to have the baby," he wrote. "But it made no sense at all. We were both children ourselves."

Mickey had gotten to know Lana during her first film at MGM, *Love Finds Andy Hardy*, which was being cast when she signed her contract. Judy Garland made her debut in a Hardy film as Betsy Booth, who always managed to get Andy out of trouble. Lana played a schoolgirl who was dynamite in a bathing suit but never got her hair wet. She enjoyed smooching so much, Andy had to ask his father, Judge Hardy, how to keep cool under the fire of her kisses.

An Andy Hardy movie was an excellent vehicle for an up-and-coming starlet. Mickey Rooney always stole the show, but audiences looked forward to his latest puppy-love crushes. Lana was one of them, as were Esther Williams, Donna Reed, Ann Rutherford, Kathryn Grayson, and Bonita Granville.

Lana's next film for MGM was *The Chaser*, but her one scene with Dennis O'Keefe was cut out. Lana was seen only briefly, sitting with her legs crossed in her attorney's waiting room, wearing an elaborate hat. In 1938 Lana also played a frisky teenager in *Rich Man, Poor Girl*, with Robert Young and Lew Ayres, followed by *Dramatic School*, produced by Mervyn LeRoy. This story about a group of aspiring young actresses starred Luise Rainer and Paulette Goddard; Lana's part was a small one, but she received fourth billing.

Lana's big break came when she was chosen as one of Clark Gable's blond chorus girls in Robert Sherwood's *Idiot's Delight*, filmed in 1938 and released the following year. Lana was not happy about bleaching her hair, but there was no arguing with the studio; contract players did what they were told. But she never made it into *Idiot's Delight*. Instead she was hospitalized for the removal of

scar tissue from her ovaries and colon, the result of a
botched appendectomy at the age of fourteen. The operation described by Lana was by no means an emergency,
and MGM gave her a bonus. This led to speculation that
she was the chorus girl who was fired by Carole Lombard
for trying to make out with her husband, Clark Gable. The
few people who claim she was the one base their opinion
on the fact that *Idiot's Delight* was Lana's big chance. Then
there was the theory that she was withdrawn from the film
because her grades in school were so bad. The reason is
not as important as the fact that Lana became a blonde.
This not only changed Lana's screen image but gave her
such an outgoing, swinging personality that Hollywood
called her the Nightclub Queen.

Mildred was very upset that Lana went out every night
and barely made it home in time to change clothes before
rushing to the studio. She always looked rested and radiant,
however. Louis B. Mayer was fond of Lana, but when
Mildred failed to discipline her, he took over. It was important, he stressed, that she not be seen drinking and
smoking in nightclubs. So far MGM had been able to air-
brush out any cocktail glasses and cigarettes, but Mayer
said it was impossible to fix every picture taken of her at
Ciro's and the Trocadero. A clean, all-American image was
important to MGM.

Lana pouted and Mayer shed a tear. He understood
his young players all too well. Having fun was part of growing up, but sweet young ladies did not go out dancing every
night with a different man. Nor did they drink and smoke.
Then Lana shed a tear, and he consoled her with compliments. She thanked him and went about her business,
living it up on the nightclub circuit.

Mayer called Lana back to his office, but this time he
summoned Mildred too. Why was she defying him? Dis-

appointing him? Risking her career? He wept, Lana sobbed, and Mildred sniffled. It's been said that Louis B. Mayer was the best actor at MGM, and though he was usually sincere, the mogul could shed a tear if the occasion warranted. Once he had made his point and gotten others to weep in their own defense, Mayer sometimes moved in for the kill. His spies told him about Lana's promiscuousness, and he laid it on the line that day in front of Mildred, who was so flushed with embarrassment that she walked out with her daughter in tow.

Mayer held all the aces. In every MGM contract was a morals clause, stating that the artist had to conduct him- or herself with due respect to public conventions and morals; he or she would not do anything or commit any act that would degrade him or her in society. In 1938 America's morals were strict, and movies, particularly those at MGM, abided by the rules that society dictated.

Lana Turner was not an established star as yet. Though some fan mail was trickling in, she had not proved her worth. Dozens of girls who were just as pretty and with more talent were being dropped every week from all the studios. Lana might have been flighty, but she wasn't stupid, so for a while she behaved herself. Mayer, in turn, reminded her that fame and fortune were just around the corner if she maintained a clean reputation and worked hard.

After producing *The Wizard of Oz* at MGM, Mervyn LeRoy realized how much he missed sitting in the director's chair. He would do many films for Metro over the years, but at the beginning of 1939 he decided to become a freelance director. Before leaving MGM, he asked agent Johnny Hyde to represent Lana in negotiating a new contract, for

$250 a week. She hired a maid, then bought a new car and wardrobe for herself and Mildred, who was no longer working.

MGM press agent George Nichols said, "Lana was always very nice to everyone. She liked being primped and pampered. Before she became a star, Lana enjoyed being one. She liked money, men, and elegant living . . . clothes and jewelry. Lana didn't have to use men, per se. Whether she was intimate with them or not, they were nuts about her. Lana liked sex, believe me, but she didn't have to use the casting couch to get ahead. I never knew if there was anything between her and LeRoy. After his divorce in the late thirties, he got around. Mervyn was a good-looking guy and he adored Lana. I feel, however, that he thought of her as the shy little girl who auditioned for him and needed protecting. Benny Thau was head of talent at MGM and the guy to seduce if a gal wanted to get beyond the front gate. Benny was nuts about Lana, but she didn't have to play the game because she was Mervyn's protégée, and Mayer respected Mervyn. These men were gentlemen, and Lana didn't play around with gentlemen. One of her dates was an actor who never amounted to anything. He told me she was oversexed. I asked him what was wrong with that, and he replied, 'Because Lana comes on like a romantic teenager and then turns into a feverish, passionate tiger who can't get enough.' Mayer knew this and kept an eye on her, as he did Judy Garland and so many others who were forever falling in love and getting pregnant. If he made threats, it was for their own good, because Mayer would do anything to help them."

Another popular series of MGM films was about young Dr. Kildare (played by Lew Ayres) and his elder mentor, Dr.

Gillespie (Lionel Barrymore). These movies, like the Andy Hardy films, were good vehicles for beginners, and Lana was pressed into service. In 1939 she appeared in *Calling Dr. Kildare*, playing the sister of a racketeer who is shot. Dr. Kildare saves his life but does not report it to the police because he is smitten with Lana. He almost loses his medical license, but she finally comes forth with the truth.

Lana played a gangster's moll in the film, living in luxury with her diamonds and furs. She tells Kildare, "I like big shiny limousines and orchids." This was Lana's first major role, the one that proved she was perfect as a haughty gold-digger with a warm heart. She received fifth billing in *Calling Dr. Kildare* and was briefly mentioned in the reviews.

Lana tried out for the part of Scarlett O'Hara in *Gone with the Wind*. Not considered a serious contender, she said later, "To my horror, they showed the auditions on TV, mine included, and I was certainly no threat to Vivien Leigh!"

Chapter 3

✳ FIRST LOVE ✳

In 1939 LANA FELL IN LOVE WITH A THIRTY-year-old attorney, Gregson Bautzer. He was tall, tanned, handsome, brilliant, wealthy, and single. Charming and sophisticated, he swept Lana off her feet without taking advantage of her youth and supposed innocence. They were seen everywhere together—at private parties, nightclubs, and Hollywood premieres. Mayer was delighted. He admired Bautzer's legal tactics and considered him a rare catch for any woman. And it goes without saying that Mildred was thrilled to find out Greg was interested in Lana, taking her out regularly, getting her home at a reasonable hour, and ending the evening with only a goodnight kiss at the front door.

Lana insisted she was a virgin when she met Bautzer and claimed he was a gentleman until she was ready and willing. After she was intimate with him, Lana expected marriage, but there was no hint of a proposal. To pacify her Greg gave Lana a small diamond ring, and she took it for granted that they were engaged.

Lana did not press the issue of marriage just yet, because MGM made it clear to her that, single and available, she was a good investment; married, her male fans might lose interest. That was the studio system, and though difficult to believe, it was also the attitude of moviegoers who did not want their fantasies shattered.

Lana saw Greg regularly, but she was extremely busy making films, one after the next. Then there were acting lessons, posing for publicity photos, learning her lines, and rehearsing. She was cast as the leading lady in *These Glamour Girls* and became determined to live up to her star billing.

When Lana received a phone call from Joan Crawford, she thought nothing of it because she and Greg had attended several of Joan's parties. "Why don't you come over to my place for tea and a chat, dear?" Joan purred.

Lana thought that would be very nice, and it was for the first few minutes. Joan made sure her guest was comfortable and fawned over Lana, who regarded this attention from a big movie star as rather flattering until Joan began lecturing her about the deceptions that were so common in Hollywood, particularly in the romance department. "I should know," Joan sighed. "That's why I think it's best if you face a few facts even though they're hurtful ones."

"I don't understand," Lana said.

"Greg doesn't love you. He loves me. We love each other, in fact, and it's been like this for a long time." Joan looked at her blond victim with a sad smile and continued on about Greg's innocent flirtations that should not be taken seriously. "You're young, my dear, but you'll get over it. I'm telling you this because Greg doesn't quite know how to tell you."

Lana tried to tell her she didn't believe it, but Joan didn't give her a chance to say much of anything. "So, Lana dear, why don't you be a good girl and tell him you're finished—that you know the truth now, and it's over. Make it easier on yourself, because he doesn't want to hurt you."

Stunned, hurt, and humiliated, Lana managed to hold back the tears and appear cool. But she felt sick, and her heart was pounding. Her only thought was to get away from Joan. She wasted no time in confronting Greg, who denied everything. But Lana had to face certain facts. He had been with many women and was accustomed to a bed partner who was exciting, stimulating, and satisfying—à la Joan Crawford. It also occurred to her that he caroused after dropping her off early if she had to work the next morning.

When Greg was not at home the evening she called, it was devastating. But she still loved him and hoped her suspicions were wrong. Lana buried herself in her role of a dance-hall girl involved with a wealthy Ivy Leaguer (played by Lew Ayres) in *These Glamour Girls*. Shunned by the debutantes in his snooty group, she takes over by entertaining the group with a wild dance at an exclusive house party. The boys gravitate to her, the debs hate her, and she wins the unspoiled and clean-cut young college senior.

The *New York Times* wrote, "We like everything about *These Glamour Girls*, and we like Lana Turner." The review went on to say the film was "the best social comedy of the year." The *London Evening News* said that Lana— "beautiful, full of life, impish and sensitive"—was "now well on her way to stardom."

Greg Bautzer faded out of Lana's life. He continued seeing Joan Crawford for years, and theirs was a torrid on-and-off-again love affair. One of Greg's habits was climbing up a rose trellis to Joan's bedroom in the middle of the night. Once he fell and broke his leg. Joan confided to a friend that it was very romantic when Greg forced his way into her bedroom after an argument. But the long affair ended when he danced with another woman at a party. Joan was very sweet about it and offered to drive him home. In the middle of nowhere, she stopped the car. "I think I might have a flat tire," she said. "Darling, do you mind getting out and taking a look?" He did, and she drove off, leaving Greg in a haze of dust three miles out of town.

Lana and Greg continued to see each other, but she had given up any thought of marriage. It took a long time for her to get Bautzer out of her system. When she did go out with someone else, a cozy table in the corner or a romantic song would remind her of Greg.

Lana went back to the nightclub scene with many men, including George Raft and Victor Mature, but she was also paying close attention to her career. Lana was on the brink of becoming a major star. It was probably her frustration over Bautzer that prompted Lana to stand up to Mayer during the shooting of *These Glamour Girls*. She demanded a dressing room of her own and got it. Perhaps Mayer was one step ahead of her, because in *Dancing Co-ed* she got top billing for the first time.

Lana played a professional dancer who enrolls at a Midwestern college to get publicity as the winner of a rigged dance contest. By the time the editor of the school newspaper (played by Richard Carlson) discovers the movie studio's plot, he and Lana have fallen in love, and she gives up her career for marriage.

Bandleader Artie Shaw appears as himself in *Dancing Co-ed*. He was America's King of Swing, making his first appearance on the screen, but he was not popular at the studio. Lana thought he was very egotistical and stayed clear of him except for her dance routines. Shaw considered Hollywood beneath him and complained about his dialogue, his makeup, and camera angles. Lana remembered him spending most of the time primping. "And that was funny," she said, "because he wasn't any too good-looking to begin with." Artie didn't have anything nice to say about her either.

Dancing Co-ed got good reviews, but it was Lana whom the critics applauded. She was now a full-fledged star, they agreed, and going places fast. Lana's success was sealed when she made the cover of *Life* and *Time* magazines.

Success gave Lana the self-confidence she'd never had. It was evident on the screen, and she also used it to show Greg that fame meant more to her than he did. But if Mildred had her way, Lana would be a great star and married to Bautzer as well. (There would be security for her as well with this arrangement.)

Six months after the completion of *Dancing Co-ed*, comedian Phil Silvers invited Artie Shaw onto the set of *Two Girls on Broadway*, where Lana, wearing a revealing green satin gown, was rehearsing. Shaw didn't recognize her at first, but he liked what he saw. She approached him, saying, "Remember me?" He sure did and waited for her to make a snide remark or walk away. Instead, Lana flirted and hinted at wanting a date. Shaw suggested dinner some time and she gave him her phone number.

On February 12, 1940, Mildred's birthday, Greg had invited her and Lana for dinner. At the last minute he called to cancel the date. "I have stomach problems," he said. Apparently Lana was used to these excuses, because she was furious, not worried. A few minutes later Artie called, and Lana went out with him alone. They drove along the ocean, talking. Artie said he was surprised that the beautiful vision sitting next to him wanted a home and babies. It appeared that Lana was honestly expressing her most secret desires. She was, however, thinking aloud about the kind of life she wanted with Bautzer.

Artie said Lana reeked of sincerity as she bared her soul to him—how she yearned for a husband and child. He began to wonder if a marriage to her would work out.

Lana claimed in her autobiography, however, that it was Artie who talked about wanting to settle down in a little house with a wife and lots of children. He was tired of running and needed someone to come home to.

As Lana listened, she changed her mind about Artie. He was a nice guy after all and too shy to propose to her.

"Let's go," she said.

That they never got around to having dinner is one thing, but not sealing the "marriage proposal" with a kiss is almost laughable. Looking back, Lana said she did it to spite Bautzer. As for Artie, who'd already been divorced twice, he described marriage as one way to get a girl into bed!

They rushed back to Shaw's house where he called a pilot, Paul Mantz, and told him to get his plane ready for a round-trip flight to Las Vegas. The cab driver, who met them at the airport, called George E. Marshall, Justice of the Peace, who greeted them at the door in a bathrobe. After the brief ceremony, Artie took off his blue star sapphire ring and put it on Lana's finger. Then the bride and groom kissed for the first time.

Before flying home, Lana sent a telegram to her mother, saying that she had eloped to Las Vegas without mentioning the groom's name. Mildred thought it could be Bautzer and, if so, his servants might have some information. Greg answered the phone and Mildred read Lana's telegram. "Did she go out with anyone last night?" he asked. When Mildred mentioned Shaw, Bautzer did some fast investigating and then confirmed the truth to a shocked and disappointed Mildred.

Reporters were waiting at Shaw's house. Lana was tense, but MGM had taught her to always be polite to the press by answering a few questions or making a brief statement. Artie, however, was furious. He raged at the newsmen, called them names, and came close to using his fists. Lana waved courteously as Artie dragged her to the front door, which he slammed and bolted. But the reporters banged on all the doors and broke windows. Lana begged Artie to let her talk to them briefly and set up a press conference for the next day—anything to placate them. But Artie wouldn't let her. In desperation, Lana called MGM's head of publicity, Howard Strickling, who sent members of his staff to deal with the press.

Finally, the bride and groom escaped to the house of a friend for their wedding night. Exhausted, Lana hoped to get some rest. She did, but not before Artie had consummated their marriage. It was quick and unromantic. When he turned his back and went to sleep, Lana thought about Greg.

Louis B. Mayer was furious. He told Lana he was very, very disappointed and gave her only three days for a honeymoon. He also warned Lana, "For heaven's sake, don't get pregnant," and he told Artie to use condoms, by all means.

Reporters approached Bautzer about his girlfriend's elopement: "I'm really heartbroken. This came as a great surprise to me," he said.

Pinup girl Betty Grable said about Artie, "That son of a bitch! Who does he think he is, doing that to me!" Then

Betty, who thought *she* was engaged to Artie, aborted his baby.

Judy Garland wept. She too had dated the bandleader shortly before he'd eloped with Lana and was under the impression he was serious about her.

Artie's line about wanting to settle down where it's peaceful and quiet with a wife and lots of kiddies was well known. It would work eight times. When a friend referred to him as a wolf, Artie said, "Well, I'm not a wolf. I marry 'em. It must be evident to you by now that nobody is more eager in a search for a happy married life than I am."

Artie's relationship with women was complex. He demanded perfection but always managed to find at least one flaw. "Green's not your color *either*" was a teaser to a girl wearing pink. Was it a comment or an insult? Most women wanted to find out. Artie was able to back up his good looks with impeccable grammar and a knowledge of current affairs and ancient history. While he talked or listened, one got the feeling he was thinking about something far beyond the limited scope of most.

Was his subconscious aim to change all females because he had little respect for his widowed Jewish mother? Only his analyst knows for sure.

Chapter 4

✳ FAME AND FREEDOM ✳

ARTIE SHAW WAS BORN ARTHUR ARSHAW-sky in the Bronx in 1910. He grew up on New York City's Lower East Side with his overly possessive widowed mother, whom he loathed. During an argument she once threatened to jump out the window. Artie said he walked across the street so he could watch her do it.

By the age of twenty he was already one of the most gifted bandleaders and swing clarinetists in America. This tall, dark, suave, well-read intellectual was a sheer genius in all his endeavors, except marriage.

Artie was an irresistible Don Juan. He charmed and seduced some of the most beautiful women in America. But he had an ego to match his sex appeal, an ego that was overbearing.

Before Judy Garland made *The Wizard of Oz*, she met and fell in love with Shaw. While MGM's seventeen-year-old Dorothy was skipping down the Yellow Brick Road with a tin man, a lion, and a scarecrow, Artie was "beginning the beguine" with Betty Grable, who was planning to marry him after her divorce from Jackie Coogan. It was Betty's misfortune (or was it?) that she had to wait a year before her final decree.

There is little information about Shaw's first two wives. Judy Carns, of Ashtabula, Ohio, was so young her parents had the marriage annulled in 1932. His second, Margaret Allen, a New York nurse, divorced him for infidelity in 1937 after he'd been caught in a hotel room with another woman. The decree made it illegal for him to ever remarry in New York.

There are no adjectives to properly describe Artie Shaw. Possibly he was too learned and was too eager to change the world. One would never have suspected this to watch him on the bandstand.

MGM arranged for an informal press conference at Artie's house the morning after the wedding. While Lana, who had no change of clothing, tried to pull herself together, Artie handed her a lead pencil and said sternly, "Put on your eyebrows."

After the newlyweds had met with reporters, Lana went home to get some clothes. Mildred asked her why she'd married Shaw and the answer was "Because I think he'll make me happy." After loading the car with her belongings, Lana returned to Artie, who took one look at her collection of shoes and had a tantrum. True to form, the bride painted her face and put on an expensive daytime frock. Artie told her to change into a simple blouse, skirt, and flat heels. "And take off your lipstick!" he shouted.

Shaw also expected his wife to clean house, do the washing, and cook his meals. In their spare time, he chose good books for her to absorb. Lana tried her hand at cooking, but the worst was rushing home from the studio every evening. Artie expected her to be there when he walked in the door.

After two months of marriage, Lana was shocked to find out she was the third Mrs. Shaw, but she blamed herself for marrying a man she knew nothing about. That

Artie was the master of the house was all right with her. He resented Mildred and refused to let her in the house if she didn't give him plenty of notice in advance. Artie obviously didn't like Mama Turner, and the feeling was mutual.

Two Girls on Broadway is the story of two sisters who fall in love with the same man (George Murphy). Joan Blondell bows out of the triangle, and Lana gets her guy. Critics liked the film and raved about Lana's dance routine with Murphy to the tune of "My Wonderful One, Let's Dance." Most reviews hinted that no movie could be bad if Lana Turner was in it.

MGM then rushed her into *We Who Are Young*. Lana played a young girl who marries impulsively. (The plot was too close to home in Artie's opinion.) She and her husband (John Shelton) are so poor he has to steal a car to get his pregnant wife to the hospital in time to give birth.

During the filming of *We Who Are Young*, Artie insisted on a New York honeymoon. MGM threatened to suspend Lana without pay, but they changed their mind when her agent, Johny Hyde, intervened. Lana's fans were waiting in New York, but Artie made her promise: "No interviews and no autographs." This was not an easy feat. While he pulled and tugged her away from avid admirers, Lana threw kisses and apologized. Artie said she wasn't obligated to them in any way.

Columnist Louella Parsons wrote that Lana would have defied MGM and a most promising career by going to New York to please Artie. Parsons said Lana used her heart instead of her head, adding, "Of course, she's very young and trusting."

Though Lana knew she had made a mistake as early as three days after eloping, she managed to stay with Artie for four months. She said he once threw her home-cooked dinner on the floor in front of guests. "What is this crap?" he growled. "Clean it up!"

The end came one morning in June 1940. Artie told Lana to have his shoes shined. "I have an early call at the studio," she said in a rush. He left the house before she did. His last words were "Have those shoes shined!"

Lana picked up the telephone and called Greg Bautzer about getting a divorce. "Pack up your things," he said, "and I'll get you out of there today."

To gain public sympathy, MGM sent Lana on a cruise to Hawaii with one of their trusted publicists, Betty Asher. According to Metro, Lana was in a "highly emotional state" and close to a nervous collapse when her marriage broke up. Actually, Lana wasn't a bit concerned—until, that is, she found out she was pregnant. Her only consolation was that the divorce wasn't yet final, but when she called Artie, he wanted to know "Who's the father?"

"You, of course!" she screamed on the phone.

"It's not mine," Artie said. Apparently he was well aware that she had been seeing other men.

But their stories differ.

Artie stated that Lana only confided in Louis B. Mayer and Johnny Hyde. She was hospitalized for "nervous exhaustion." In other words, she aborted the baby.

Artie insisted he knew nothing about Lana's pregnancy, although he suspected something because he knew she was not having a nervous breakdown. "Lana wasn't the type," he said.

When Artie found out the truth from a friend, he remarked that all along she'd had no intention of having children. Lana's only ambition was becoming a big star.

Artie did say, however, that he considered marrying her again. Lana came to his house frequently and would spend the night with him. On these occasions they didn't argue and he made no demands on her, so they got along very well. But Artie could not deny the truth: He was a realist, and Lana lived in a dream world.

Tony Martin was a dreamy-eyed crooner recently divorced from actress Alice Fay. He was one of Lana's "steady" dates in public. Fan magazines reported that Martin gave her laughter and happiness at a time when she needed it, and that she sought his counsel and advice. Lana said in an interview, "I just know that everything in my life has changed. I have found myself." Then there was the handsome hunk Victor Mature, on whom Lana set her sights— again. She was seen with Greg Bautzer, too, bandleader Tommy Dorsey, and drummers Buddy Rich and Gene Krupa.

Lana testified in divorce court that Artie embarrassed her in front of his friends because she "was dull but couldn't help it." She told Superior Judge Thomas C. Gould that Artie would stay out all night and not tell her where he had been.

"Did you try to get along with your husband, madam?" Gould asked.

"I tried everything."

"His complaint was that you were coming home from the studio at 8:30 P.M."

"Yes," Lana replied.

"And did he refuse to eat dinner with you?"

"Yes."

"You made a sincere effort to make a go of your marriage?"

"Yes, because I wanted my marriage to be a success."

This testimony was typical of Hollywood divorces. The same simple question was asked by the judge over and over, so that his "divorce granted" was justified.

Lana was earning almost a thousand dollars a week at MGM and did not ask for alimony. She assumed Artie would allow her to take the expensive baby grand piano that had been a wedding present from Mildred. He kept it and refused to discuss the matter.

About her marriage to Artie, Lana said, "He was my college education."

Artie said her remark was nonsense because Lana had no interest in expanding her knowledge. He implied that she lacked depth and wasn't very bright. After his eighth marriage Shaw advised, "If divorce is inevitable, my advice is to call a cab. A lawyer will do the rest."

MGM was anxious to cash in on the publicity generated by Lana's brief marriage to the King of Swing. *The Great Ziegfeld* had been such a colossal success in 1936 that Mayer wanted to do a sequel right away starring Joan Crawford. Production of *Ziegfeld Girl* was postponed until 1941, and Lana was cast as the doomed showgirl who cannot cope with fame and adulation. She snubs her beau (played by James Stewart), becomes an alcoholic, and dies at the end. Though Lana had handled some serious acting roles well, her part in *Ziegfeld Girl* had more depth. Judy Garland and Hedy Lamarr co-starred in this extravaganza of fabulous costumes and sets, lively music, and beautiful women. (Lana got fourth billing, after Stewart, Garland, and Lamarr.)

Lana's part was originally a small one, but director Robert Z. Leonard handed her new pages of dialogue every day, explaining that he was expanding her role of the doomed Sheila. Fortunately, Lana was able to learn her lines quickly for *Ziegfeld Girl*.

The *New York Times* raved about two musical numbers, "You Stepped Out of a Dream" and "I'm Always Chasing Rainbows," and wrote, "The girls, especially Lana Turner, who must have been born on Olympus, are breathtaking. She gives a surprisingly solid performance."

MGM put a star on Lana Turner's dressing-room door and increased her salary to $1,500 a week, and President Roosevelt introduced himself to her at his White House birthday party.

Lana was dating her co-star in *Ziegfeld Girl*, Jimmy Stewart, who was an eligible bachelor and much sought after by the ladies in Hollywood. Tony Martin also appeared in the film, so Lana's social life was as thrilling as her blossoming career.

After the Artie Shaw fiasco, Mildred and Lana gave up their small apartments and moved into a beautiful house in Benedict Canyon. Both women were spendthrifts and, according to Mayer, Lana was usually in debt. But she always managed to rise above it all on her own by sheer hard work.

Following his divorce from Lana, Artie was stricken with granulocytophenia, a rare blood disease that weakens the white cells and is often fatal. He fought it and recovered just in time for America's entry into World War II. Still weak, he joined the navy and toured military bases with his band in the South Seas and Australia. In 1944 Artie collapsed both mentally and physically and was granted a military discharge. "I was in a state of dysfunction," he said. "I was nowhere.

In desperation he turned to psychoanalyst May Romm, whom he visited three times a week. But Artie's impudence and conceit undoubtedly nourished his pride. He reorganized a band and began to get his life in order with Romm's help. In 1945 he married luscious Ava Gardner, whom Artie forced into therapy with Romm. He also insisted she take college courses and wear her shoes in the house. (Ava liked to walk in her bare feet.) There was also the "no lipstick" law. During a trip to New York, Artie caught Ava reading the novel *Forever Amber* and he promptly threw it out. Ironically, he would later marry Kathleen Winsor, the author this sizzling book.

Lana's next film was *Dr. Jekyll and Mr. Hyde*, with Spencer Tracy and Ingrid Bergman. Lana was originally set to play the part of Hyde's abused barmaid, whom he kills, but Tracy asked director Victor Fleming to give Bergman the bigger part. Lana was cast instead as Jekyll's well-bred fiancée. She had very little to do other than wear elegant gowns and look beautiful.

Dr. Jekyll and Mr. Hyde was Ingrid Bergman's fourth American film, but it was her next one, *Casablanca*, that launched her career. She was married to Petter Lindstrom at the time and had a daughter, Pia, but Ingrid was having a torrid affair with director Victor Fleming. Spencer Tracy fell in love with her instantly. Sparks flew on the set of *Dr. Jekyll and Mr. Hyde* when Ingrid got involved with Spencer. Whether Tracy's doomed romance with Bergman had anything to do with his bad behavior, no one knows. An alcoholic, he went into a deep state of depression when the film failed at the box office. Tracy then met Katharine Hepburn and the rest of that story is history.

Lana insisted she did not want the part of the barmaid-prostitute because it was too difficult for her. But there are too many reliable sources who say that Fleming and Tracy went to bat for Bergman. Lana got third billing and was barely mentioned in the reviews.

Chapter 5

✳ GABLE AND TAYLOR ✳

CLARK GABLE WAS DISSATISFIED WITH HIS films after *Gone with the Wind* in 1939. MGM paired him with Hedy Lamarr in *Comrade X* and Rosalind Russell in *They Met in Bombay*, but Gable considered these properties only fair. He liked a script called *Honky Tonk*, about a ruthless gambler in the old West. His wife, Carole Lombard, thought it was a lousy idea and L. B. Mayer agreed, but Gable was determined and asked his good friend Jack Conway to direct the movie. MGM offered to find something better, but Clark said he had more faith in a good director than a good script. Conway, a hearty drinker and womanizer, had worked with Gable on five films, including *Saratoga* and *Boom Town*.

"I know I'm stickin' my neck out on this one," Clark told Carole, "but I'm gonna fight for it." He remained adamant about *Honky Tonk* and wanted to begin production right away. Mayer relented and chose Lana as Gable's leading lady.

Carold Lombard saw red when she heard the news. She said that Lana's role as the sweet young Bostonian virgin in *Honky Tonk* did not reflect Miss Turner's reputation. Clark Gable was Lana's first famous leading man, and after a few days of filming *Honky Tonk,* rumors of a romance were so rampant that Carole threatened to confront the "lovers" on the set and "kick them both in the ass." Her fights with Clark were bitter and explosive. "I'll have her fired!" she told him.

"You can't do that," he argued.

"Then I'll have you fired!"

Carole went directly to Mayer and threatened to keep Clark from reporting to work if Lana tried to "get her hands on him." A quiet alert was called on the set of *Honky Tonk* whenever Carole drove through the MGM studio gates. Her visits ceased after Lana, rehearsing a scene with Clark, spotted Carole and ran to her dressing room in tears. From then on the set was off limits to outsiders, including Mrs. Gable.

Lana described how she glanced over her shoulder and saw Carole glaring at her. "I felt faint and walked away. Jack Conway came to my dressing room and asked me to come back, but I told him I couldn't do that. I had to get hold of myself. My knees were shaking. Finally someone knocked on my door and told me it was time to resume work. Carole Lombard was gone."

Lana apologized to Clark, who whispered, "I understand, honey."

Columnist Sheila Graham later commented, "I wish movie queens would tell the truth or shut up. Reading Lana's memoirs, I got the impression she was a candidate for the convent."

Gable had hundreds of women, and though he loved Carole Lombard, that didn't stop him from playing around. He was a humble guy, but he would tell his cronies that he'd been intimate with most of his leading ladies. If they weren't available, he played with a pretty extra. Myrna Loy, one of Clark's frequent co-stars, pushed him off her front porch when he tried to get fresh. (At the time, his second wife, Ria, was waiting in the car.) Loy said Gable ignored her after that, playing up to other women on the movie set. Though he wasn't a conceited fellow, Gable had his reputation to think about. Though his fans thought he was a great lover, Carole Lombard said, "God knows I love Clark, but he's the worst lay in town." Joan Crawford had a long affair with him and echoed Carole's words. Gable had hundreds of flings that meant nothing more to him than morale boosters.

But there was a chemistry between Clark and Lana on and off the screen. Mayer, however, kept an eye on the situation because he did not want his two top stars getting involved. Ten years earlier, Mayer had threatened to ruin the careers of Gable and Crawford if they continued seeing each other on the sly.

Lana was in awe of Gable at first, but their fervent love scenes cured her within days. Mayer, however, demanded that *Honky Tonk* be finished in short order to separate Turner and Gable, who were so hot on the screen, the studio could not overlook the possibilities of pairing them again in the near future.

At the premiere of *Honky Tonk*, Clark and Carole snuggled and held hands in the theater. Observers said he was somewhat embarrassed that his wife was overly doting in public.

Gable's hunches about *Honky Tonk* were right. He and Lana, who got equal billing, made the cover of *Life* magazine together as the "hot new team." Their roles could have been written for them: Clark as the rowdy gambler Candy Johnson, and Lana as Elizabeth Cotton, a little lady from Boston. He wants to play games with her, but she gets him drunk and the next morning he wakes up with a hangover and a wedding ring. Their marriage is rocky, but Lana proves she can hold her own with the saloon girls *and* hold on to her husband.

Honky Tonk commanded only good reviews. *Variety* summed them up: "Miss Turner, who is graced by tremendous sex appeal, proves she can act as well as turn the boys on. She clicks with Gable in this lusty Western that makes you wish you were there."

Lana was then rushed into *Johnny Eager* with Robert Taylor, Van Heflin, who won an Oscar for best supporting actor, and Edward Arnold. Taylor told a close friend, "Lana wasn't very career-minded, and preferred men and jewelry over anything else. She wasn't as 'busty' as her pinup pictures, but her face was delicate and beautiful. I've never seen lips like hers, and though I was not one to run after blondes, Lana was the exception. I couldn't take my eyes off her, and there were times during *Johnny Eager* that I thought I'd explode. She had a voice like a breathless child. I don't think she knew how to talk without being sexy. When she said 'Good morning,' I melted. She was the kind of woman a guy would risk five years in jail for rape."

Acting daily with Lana frustrated Taylor. He took it as long as he could, and when he discovered she was making no effort to ignore his attentions and was physically drawn to him, he had to have her, "if only for one night." Their affair went beyond that, however, because Bob asked his wife, Barbara Stanwyck, for a divorce so he could marry Lana. The Taylors separated for a few days and reconciled in name only. Barbara never spoke to Lana again.

Press agent George Nichols said Turner did not want to be responsible for Bob's divorce. "MGM would not permit it," Nichols said. "Taylor wasn't the type to take divorce in stride, so if he asked Barbara for his freedom, Bob knew what he was doing."

I asked Nichols if it was possible that Lana went from Gable to Taylor. "Sure," he replied. "We used to kid around about Clark and Bob sharing the same girls. They were close buddies, but Bob was modest by saying he got Clark's leftovers. The truth is that Gable gave Taylor phone numbers of the girls he was no longer seeing. I don't think Clark's marriage to Carole was in trouble, but Bob and Barbara were forced to get married after a three-year courtship. MGM saw a scandal brewing and rushed them to the altar. Taylor was Mayer's favorite, but it's hard to say what might have happened if Lana wanted to marry Bob. My guess is that Mayer would have talked Taylor out of it—father to son."

Johnny Eager, directed by Mervyn LeRoy, is excellent entertainment, and it stands up today with the best gangster films. Taylor, in the title role, falls in love with the daughter of a district attorney, a doomed affair that gets him killed in the end.

Critics said that Lana Turner and Robert Taylor were the most striking couple on the screen. They played well together, and MGM wanted to team them again, but it never happened.

After Bob and Barbara Stanwyck were divorced in 1952 and he had remarried, Lana was at the opening of a hotel in Lake Tahoe. When she heard that Barbara was there also, Lana called to invite her for a drink. The answer was an icy negative. Stanwyck was a lady who held a grudge, especially if it involved her one and only, Robert Taylor, whom she worshiped to her dying day. She disliked every woman he dated after their divorce and displayed her feelings openly.

There were rumors that Stanwyck tried to cut her wrist after Taylor had confessed his love for Lana. Barbara was rushed to the hospital, claiming she'd tried to open a window and accidently put her arm through the pane. Hollywood insiders were quick to pick up on this, even though Stanwyck was not the suicide type. Her press agent, Helen Ferguson, said, "I think Barbara might have been drinking when she had the accident. She drank too much if times were good, so one can only imagine how much she consumed when times were bad."

Lana and Taylor remained friends, however. Bob remarried in 1954, and he and his new wife, Ursula, socialized with Lana and her fourth husband, Lex Barker. A drunken Stanwyck once made an embarrassing scene when she arrived uninvited at a dinner party to "get a look at Bob's German wife." Barker rose to the occasion and took Barbara firmly by the arm, escorting her out the door.

By now Lana's power over men was well known in Hollywood. Carole Lombard could not let her guard down after *Hony Tonk* because Lana and Clark were under contract to MGM and on the same lot every day. Carole knew about the Turner-Taylor involvement. Everyone in Hollywood loved to gossip, and Lombard was the champ. She was never malicious and only talked to people she trusted. Occasionally Carole was known to chat with columnists "off the cuff," as she did about Gable's endowments and his ineptness in the bedroom. Reporters noted in particular that it was very unusual for Gable to attend premieres. If MGM didn't force him to go to the opening of *Honky Tonk*, who did? Carole, of course, with her arm wrapped around his and traces of lipstick on his neck after the movie.

But a few weeks later, Lombard went into a rage when she found out that Clark and Lana were going to co-star in *Somewhere I'll Find You.* The bickering and battling began all over again. Gable believed that if his having affairs with other women meant nothing to him, why should it mean anything to his wife? His "logic" added fire to her fury, but she would have to live with it because MGM's demands came first.

The fact that the public clamored for more of Lana Turner in the arms of Clark Gable after *Honky Tonk* was good business. But Lombard was more concerned about their marriage than Metro's box office. She spoke about wanting a baby now more than ever before.

On December 7, 1941, Lana was having a party at her house. Her guests included Frank Sinatra and Tommy Dorsey. Mildred returned from a visit to San Francisco and, hearing the laughter and music, took Lana aside. "Don't you know Pearl Harbor was bombed? We're at war."

Hollywood was just another town of Americans anxious to volunteer for the war effort. The stars got involved with the Hollywood Victory Committee, and Clark Gable was appointed chairman of the Screen Actors Division. He told Carole, "I'm gonna volunteer."

"You're almost forty-one," she said.

"Yeah, but I can get a commission. It's a lengthy procedure and I should apply for it right away."

Carole didn't want Clark to go into the service, but if he went to Washington immediately, this would prevent him from starting *Somewhere I'll Find You* with Lana in January 1942. Maybe, just maybe, she hoped, the studio would replace him.

In the meantime the Secretary of the Treasury contacted MGM's New York publicity director, Howard Dietz, about movie celebrities going on war-bond tours. Because Gable was in charge of the project, Dietz called him about Carole Lombard going to her home state of Indiana for a rally. She accepted and wanted Clark to go along, but MGM refused to postpone *Somewhere I'll Find You*, a film about war correspondents.

This was the first time the Gables would be separated, and it could not have come at a worse time. Carole did not want to leave town, but her patriotism came first. On January 12, 1942, she boarded the train with her mother, Bessie, and Gable's personal public-relations man, Otto Winkler. Clark was in Washington and due home the next day.

In Indianapolis on January 15, Carole sold more than $2 million in war bonds. After the rally she told her mother, "I'm anxious to get home to Clark. Let's fly back."

Winkler didn't like the idea and tried to talk her out of it. He was aware that Carole and Clark had quarreled bitterly over his attentions to Lana, and he thought a few days apart would be a good cooling-off period. And Winkler didn't want Gable to be caught off guard, just in case. But Carole refused to back down. "Let's flip for it," she said. They did, and she won the toss. "I don't like choo-choos," Carole said, and she made reservations on TWA. Her mother, who was a proficient numerologist, jotted down the flight data and came up with a fatal number. She showed it to Carole, who was a believer, but laughed it off. At four the next morning, January 16, they boarded the plane. She sent Clark a telegram about her change in plans, asking him to meet her at the airport that evening.

What was Gable doing while his wife was away? The press and his friends do not give the same account of what he did or where he was, other than filming *Somewhere I'll Find You*. He wasn't at the airport to meet Carole either. Her plane was delayed in Las Vegas, so Clark sent someone else to wait it out. When he couldn't be reached at home, it was MGM's publicity chief, Howard Strickling, who got the call that Carole's plane had crashed into a mountain near Las Vegas. There were no survivors.

Joan Crawford told this author that Gable came to her that night. I asked if he was with her when he got the call from Strickling, but she ignored the question. The time element is still a puzzle.

Carole's brothers never spoke to Gable again. Not only had they been deliberately eliminated from her will, but they also resented the serious quarrels over Clark's fondness for Lana, the obvious reason Carole had rushed back home to her death.

Though MGM had considered scratching *Somewhere I'll Find You*, Gable returned to work on February 23. L. B. Mayer told everyone on the set to pretend nothing had happened. Above all, no pity or tiptoeing around.

Mayer had a private talk with Lana and asked her to go along with Clark's moods. "If he wants to work, work. If he wants to leave, that's all right. If he wants to talk, talk. I hear he doesn't like to eat alone, so if he asks, join him."

Clark invited her for dinner at the ranch that he had shared with Carole. Lana said there was no mention of the tragic plane crash or his wife's death.

Gable began to drink heavily. He went into the Air Force and said, "I don't care if I ever come back." Joan

Crawford said he suffered from terrible guilt about Carole because they'd parted on a sour note, adding, "She died for love."

The plot of *Somewhere I'll Find You* revolves around war correspondents sent to Indo-China. Clark and Lana play on-and-off-again lovers who go their separate ways when World War II breaks out. Clark thinks she is dead, but he gives up his frivolous ways when they are reunited on assignment in the Philippines.

Critics applauded Gable's ability to perform so soon after his wife's death. Of Lana, they said she was another Jean Harlow. *Time* magazine wrote, "In any posture, Lana suggests she is looking up from a pillow." Actually, *Somewhere I'll Find You* is not a very good film. By the time it was released, however, news of Gable's induction in the Air Force generated publicity, and the movie made millions for MGM.

Lana sported a new short hairdo in *Somewhere I'll Find You*. A year later Veronica Lake, whose long peekaboo hairdo over one eye had made her famous as Alan Ladd's leading lady, had her locks cut, supposedly to encourage women working in defense plants to follow suit and avoid getting their hair caught in factory machinery. MGM picked up on this and claimed that Lana had sacrificed her beautiful blond hair for patriotic reasons. They were wrong in both instances, especially in Lana's case, since World War II had just begun. She did, however, go on an extensive war-bond tour, with a stopover at her birthplace, Wallace, Idaho. Lana sold kisses to anyone who bought a $50,000 bond and raised $5 million.

✻　✻　✻

In April 1942 Lana was introduced to Stephan Crane at the Mocambo nightclub. She was instantly attracted to the tall, good-looking, charming fellow who looked and talked like a millionaire. He referred to himself as Joseph Stephan Crane III, tobacco heir. As was typical of Lana, she asked no questions and did not check his credentials. Crane said he was twenty-seven, born in Indiana, and involved in several business ventures. Lana should have been suspicious after one glance at his small apartment, but she wore blinders when she was in love.

L. B. Mayer warned her about the relationship. He said Crane had close bonds with the underworld and she would surely ruin her good name by associating with gangsters. Lana listened, but she went about her business of falling deeply in love with the mysterious Crane.

Chapter 6

❋ TIE IT TIGHTER THIS TIME, JUDGE ❋

As usual, there is a "his" and "her" version of how they met. He said she sent him a note with her telephone number, and she insists they were introduced by Hyde. Who made the first move doesn't matter, because they were both capable of chasing an attractive member of the opposite sex. He was suave and polished, and she was Lana Turner.

In addition to claiming to be a tobacco heir from Indiana and a Phi Beta Kappa, Crane casually mentioned sharing a house in Malibu with department-store mogul Alfred Bloomingdale. Actually he was born Josef Stephanson Crane in 1917 and came from a middle-class family in Crawfordsville, Indiana, where his father owned a pool hall and cigar stand. In 1937 he eloped with Carol Ann Kurtz, whom he'd met in college. When his father died, young Crane took over the pool hall and lived upstairs with his bride. Two years later Carol found out Stephan was running around with other women and they separated. He went to Hollywood to make a name for himself, had his broken nose fixed, and bought a flashy car and fancy wardrobe.

Carol followed him, but the marriage was over. They signed a separation agreement in January 1941.

Stephan lived off gambling profits from the pool hall back in Indiana. As this was illegal, he collected the money in cash. This afforded him the opportunity to mingle with the right people in Hollywood's café society. He was accepted as a wealthy playboy and dated lovely starlets such as Sonja Henie, who gave lavish parties for only the elite.

Nobody in Hollywood knew much about the six-foot-two dark-haired charmer. Not even mafia boss Bugsy Siegel, who was a popular figure in the film colony, thanks to his pal George Raft and the very rich Countess de Frasso. Bugsy made a cool half million dollars shaking down studio moguls, but he was a likeable blue-eyed stud. He and Stephan became such good friends that Bugsy trusted him to squire his moll, Virginia Hill, when he was out of town. Louis B. Mayer was referring to Bugsy when he talked to Lana about Crane's gangster friends. But then many movie celebrities were seen with Seigel, because he attended premieres and was invited to private dinner parties. Lana was seen dancing with Bugsy on more than one occasion, and Mayer could do nothing about it.

Three months after Lana met Crane, they eloped to Las Vegas and were married on July 17, 1942, by the same justice of the peace who'd gotten out of bed to tie the knot for Lana and Artie Shaw. "Tie it tighter this time, Judge," the bride giggled. The next day Mildred gave the newlyweds a small reception at home.

Crane rented an apartment, but Lana thought it was too small and preferred they live at her spacious house. Once again MGM and the fan magazines had been caught off guard. Only recently Lana had been photographed nightclubbing with Tony Martin. Suddenly she was married to—Stephan who?

The studio put Lana to work in *Slightly Dangerous*, a fluffy film about a small-town girl (Lana) who poses as the long-lost daughter of a millionaire (Walter Brennan). She's exposed by her ex-boss (Robert Young), but her "adopted" father is so fond of Lana that he doesn't want to lose her. She and Young fall in love and everyone lives happily ever after.

Reviews were mild. The basic "Cinderella" theme bored the critics, who expressed their disappointment that such great performers as Walter Brennan, Dame May Whitty, Eugene Pallette, and Alan Mowbray were subjected to such nonsense. But Lana Turner had reached the status that her name on a marquee guaranteed business at the box office.

While Crane stayed home and slept late, Lana was up every morning at six o'clock for another movie, *The Youngest Profession*. The story is about a teenager (Virginia Weidler) and her adventures collecting autographs of her favorite movie stars. The cast of stars, who played themselves, was very impressive: Lana Turner, Robert Taylor, Greer Garson, Walter Pidgeon and William Powell. Reviews of *The Youngest Profession* emphasized the golden roster of stars that kept you sitting in your seat, waiting for the next one to appear. Weidler was representative of those starry-eyed youngsters who hung around railroad stations and hotels to get smiles and autographs from their Hollywood idols.

A silly plot perhaps, and yet thousands of bobby-soxers were swooning over Frank Sinatra at the Paramount Theater in New York at the time. These young girls were not only all the vogue, but they were the ones who decided which performer deserved a pedestal.

✳ ✳ ✳

Lana wondered why Crane wasn't contributing to the household expenses. Not that she needed the money, but he made no effort to pick up the tab for dinner or a night on the town. Observers said they were not affectionate in public. In fact, they seemed bored. Occasionally Lana retired early and Stephan went out alone. She seethed if he came home as she was leaving for the studio at dawn.

In November 1942, four months after the elopement, Stephan told Lana that his divorce from Carol Kurtz would not be final until after the new year. Lana was in shock and demanded to find out why Carol hadn't come forth earlier. The two women met face to face, but Lana could only find out that Crane was not free to marry for two months. He claimed ignorance, assuming he was legally divorced in January of 1941 when he'd signed the separation agreement. Lana was furious. She ordered Stephan out of the house and had all of the locks changed.

Lana was worried about what Mayer would say when he found out she was "married" to a bigamist. But there was another complicated matter: Lana found out she was pregnant. Crane pleaded with her to wait it out until they could marry again secretly, but she was hurt and fed up. MGM was powerful enough to obtain an annulment for Lana, and the judge awarded custody of her unborn baby to her. That Lana did not have an abortion proved that she hoped to reconcile with Crane, who pursued her until she agreed to go out with him again on Valentine's Day, 1943. They appeared to be a happy couple at the Mocambo. When approached by reporters, Stephan said he was optimistic about a happy ending. The next day, however, she put him off once again. Crane swallowed a handful of barbiturates, got into the car, and drove it over the cliff above Lana's house. He was taken to Cedars of Lebanon Hospital in critical condition and Lana rushed to his side. Stephan told the press he'd had a mental breakdown. Lana shed a few tears and said nothing.

A month later Crane received his draft notice and only then did Lana panic. He was marching off to battle and she was carrying his child. The least she could do was marry him again. On March 15, 1943, Lana and Stephan eloped to Tijuana, Mexico. "I stood before a little man whose office sign said 'Legal Matters Adjusted,' " she said, "and again became Stephan's wife. We called a Mexican off the street for a peso or two and made him a witness."

Crane sported a custom-made Army uniform, but he never saw active duty. The official reason was a bad back, and he received a medical discharge six months later. But it was Lana who used her influence to prevent Stephan from going overseas. Love, however, had little, if anything, to do with their remarriage and his staying close to home.

Lana needed Stephan to be with her when she gave birth to their child. And he had gotten used to the good life as the husband of a movie queen. We'll never know how much influence L. B. Mayer had over Lana during the few months she was an unwed mother-to-be. Spoiled and pampered, she got away with a great deal more than other MGM players, but Mayer had his limits. He wanted her to marry Crane again when his divorce was final, but Lana insisted she was the injured party and could never trust Stephan again. It took a good deal of sauce and sass, considering her lifestyle bordered on scandal in 1943.

Lana once said, "My life has been a series of emergencies."

One of them was the birth of Cheryl Christina on July 25, 1943. Lana's blood is Rh-negative, Cheryl's Rh-positive. The baby's blood was removed and replaced at Los Angeles Children's Hospital. Lana was anemic and forced to stay in bed without the gratification of holding her baby for three days. Mildred ran from one hospital to the other with news of Cheryl until Lana, in a wheelchair, was able to see her daughter, who had to remain in the hospital for over two months.

Lana never forgot the day she came to see Cheryl without calling the doctor ahead of time. The baby was getting a transfusion and covered with blood. Lana screamed and almost fainted. A nurse rushed her into a vacant room and explained that several needles were required for the transfusion. When they were removed, some blood would leak out. Lana just happened to walk in before the nurses had had a chance to bathe Cheryl.

Stephan had hoped for a boy. During Lana's pregnancy he would correct her reference to their baby as a "she," emphasizing that it was going to be a "he." Stephan had taken Lana to the hospital but got tired of waiting and disappeared. Lana got more support from Mildred than from her husband, but he was always available to pose for publicity photos and anxious to get back into the swing of things at Ciro's and the Mocambo. Sometimes he and Lana showed up together, but she was more often having a good time alone while Stephan was at another club enjoying himself. The good life ended when Lana realized there was no money in the bank after paying heavy medical bills. She was on leave from MGM and off their payroll temporarily. Stephan did not offer to help.

Lana knew she could make money doing radio shows, each paying around $5,000 or more. After Cheryl was safe at home and in the care of a trusted nurse, Lana headed for New York and Stephan tagged along. His excuse was that he wanted to take her to his hometown of Crawfordsville, Indiana, on the return train trip. Why Crane chose to do this when he knew his marriage was in trouble is anyone's guess.

Lana believed her husband was a tobacco heir and, as in the movies, lived in a mansion on a vast, colorful plantation. Stephan let it be known that he was coming home, and the town was thrilled to see a big limousine crawling down the main street. Instead of at a mansion, they stopped in front of an old broken-down two-story house. Lana was a good sport, and she met his mother and greeted neighbors who stayed and stared. The following day was worse. The tobacco plantation turned out to be a poolroom–cigar store. When she went inside, Lana realized that her husband was not the man she'd chosen for a husband. It wasn't so much the disappointment or the shabbiness of Stephan's roots as it was his living a lie. After all, he knew about her own humble beginnings. Whatever respect she had left for Crane was gone.

Lana returned to Hollywood eager to work, even though she hadn't fully recovered from her difficult childbirth and anemia. She had not made a film in eighteen months since a fifteen-second cameo in *DuBarry Was a Lady*, with Red Skelton, Lucille Ball, and Gene Kelly. (Lana's brief appearance was a surprise to the audience, because she did not receive any billing.)

Marriage Is a Private Affair is an artificial film. It's a dreadful bore, except for the exquisite Lana and an equally exquisite wardrobe for her part as the spoiled party girl who marries a serviceman, played by John Hodiak. But like the real Lana, her character loves to dance and have a good time. In the end, of course, she settles down happily with hubby and baby (unlike the real Lana).

Marriage Is a Private Affair had a worldwide premiere

in all theaters of the war. Preceding the movie, there was a personal filmed message from Lana to the servicemen. "You're first in our hearts," she said.

The *New York Times* wrote that the movie proved once again that "Lana Turner is a lovely, appealing little thing and that mankind was fashioned primarily to make her happy and supreme."

Lana began dating her co-star John Hodiak when her marriage to Crane was coming to an end. There were rumors that she was having an affair with Hodiak before she'd filed for divorce. Stephan refused to give Lana her freedom at first, but he had no job and no money. In April 1944, she sued Crane for divorce and was awarded custody of Cheryl. Lana testified that the marriage had been a mistake. Mildred backed up her daughter in court by telling the judge that the couple lived with her throughout their marriage. After only seven minutes, the judge granted Lana's divorce.

Hodiak wasn't the only man Lana was seeing before she broke up with Crane. Turhan Bey, the dapper Turkish actor remembered for his roles in *Arabian Nights* and *Ali Baba and the Forty Thieves*, was supposedly her favorite. They made a stunning couple, and fan magazines published nightclub photos of them. Apparently Stephan's jealousy got the best of him when he saw Lana dancing with the Turk. He broke in and demanded Lana return the diamond ring—a family heirloom—he had given to her. Bey came to Lana's defense, and the two men stepped outside to settle the matter with their fists. A distraught Lana threw the ring in the bushes, but not before Stephan received two black eyes. Bey came out of the fight with only a few bruises. This latest escapade of Lana's made the newspapers, but there was nothing unusual about two men fighting for her attention.

Stephan was embarking on a movie career of his own at Columbia Studios, and the publicity gave him a boost in *Cry of the Werewolf*. Crane got second billing to Nina Foch, but it was a forgettable film. He went from bad to worse in *Crime Doctor's Courage*. *Tonight and Every Night* did nothing for Stephan other than allow him to meet leading lady Rita Hayworth, with whom he had an affair. His tenure as an actor came to an end when he dated the girlfriend of Columbia mogul Harry Cohn, who promptly tore up Crane's contract. It was for the best, apparently, because Stephan went back to his old ways: dating wealthy women and gambling. A year later he had enough money to buy Lucy's, a popular restaurant across the street from Paramount Studios.

After her divorce from Crane, Lana was seeing so many men it's difficult to put them into proper perspective. Robert Stack, Rory Calhoun, and Ricardo Montalban were casual dates. Turhan Bey lasted quite a while, as did Victor Mature. Lana tried her best to lasso billionaire Howard Hughes, who was in the habit of chasing after women who were recently divorced, referring to them as "wet decks." Lana was supposedly engaged to him for eight hours while on a cross-country flight with Howard at the controls. She was so sure he would marry her, she had silk sheets monogrammed "HH." But Howard said he had no intention of getting married. When Lana pouted over the monogramming Hughes said, "Why don't you marry Huntington Hartford?" (Howard Hughes confirmed the validity of this story to Hollywood columnist James Bacon.)

Actor Peter Lawford, then twenty-one, fell madly in

love with Lana and claimed they were engaged to be married in 1944. Lawford's polished British accent and good looks had won him an MGM contract in 1942, but it would take him five years to achieve stardom. Peter said Lana was beautiful and famous, but she had a down-to-earth quality that won him over completely. He told friends he was madly in love with Lana and wanted to marry her. Though his impeccable good manners made Lawford appear sophisticated, he was immature and lacked the depth that Lana needed for a serious relationship. She broke his heart by dumping him for drummer Gene Krupa, a friend of Artie Shaw's. That affair was short-lived, but Lana chose not to date Peter again. His despondency made him a bitter man, and he had little respect for women after Lana told him casually on the telephone, "It's over."

In the 1950s Peter became a very successful actor and married John F. Kennedy's sister, Patricia. With his wife's money he bought L. B. Mayer's beautiful Malibu beach house, where his friend Marilyn Monroe had trysts with his brothers-in-law John and Bobby. Following Kennedy's assassination in 1963, Peter's marriage ended. He became a hopeless dope addict and died in debt. Unable to pay for a crypt, his widow was forced to remove his ashes and scatter them at sea.

Lana's next film was *Keep Your Powder Dry* with Laraine Day and Susan Peters, the story of three WACs during the war. Lana is a spoiled playgirl who enlists to prove she's worthy of an inheritance. Day is an Army brat who expects perfection, and Peters plays a young woman who joins the service to be near her husband. Lana and Laraine are at each other's throats until Susan is widowed. They all pull together and Lana decides to stay in uniform.

Though MGM made *Keep Your Powder Dry* with the assistance of the Women's Army Corps, the film was surely a glamorized version of life as a WAC. The *New York Times*'s critic Bosley Crowther referred to the movie as a "little indignity." But in 1945 Hollywood was grinding out wartime films to encourage volunteers in all branches of the service. Moviegoers left the theaters feeling very patriotic and bought defense stamps on their way out. They hated the enemy and believed Hollywood's propaganda that America was winning the war on all fronts. If nothing more, these films were great morale boosters.

Lana could do no wrong as a screen personality, nor as a twenty-five-year-old woman who was divorced twice under very unusual circumstances—having eloped with Artie Shaw on their first date and married Stephan Crane who already had a wife. But Lana's fans thought of her as an innocent victim of men who took advantage of her face and fame. The sweet image she personified was real, and audiences sensed this.

MGM was paying Lana $4,000 a week for this unique quality, not for her acting ability. The public wanted to see Lana Turner the star, not Lana Turner the actress.

Weekend at the Waldorf, a remake of 1932's *Grand Hotel* and based on a novel by Vicki Baum, was Lana's last movie of 1945. Greta Garbo's role as the lonely dancer was now played by Ginger Rogers; the newspaper correspondent originally portrayed by John Barrymore was handled with a flare of humor by Walter Pidgeon; and the role of Joan Crawford's stenographer was given to Lana. A new character was added to the cast, that of a lonely Air Force captain, played by Van Johnson. Edward Arnold is the big-time promoter who promises Lana the world that she wants: a penthouse apartment on Fifth Avenue, expensive clothes, and jewelry. She falls in love with Van Johnson and their scenes tug at the heart. But they are balanced by the amusing antics of Ginger Rogers and Walter Pidgeon.

Weekend at the Waldorf cost MGM a million dollars and broke all records at Radio City Music Hall for nine weeks. Critics said the movie was no great drama, but it was first-rate entertainment.

Lana's short "feather" hairdo became her trademark for a while. It was extremely flattering, and even though it was a popular coiffure in 1945, the hairstyle was identified with her.

Though L. B. Mayer tried his best to convince Lana that her carousing every night would ruin her reputation, she listened politely and did as she pleased. Lana occasionally dated Crane, who was still in love with her despite his numerous affairs. She leaned on Greg Bautzer for legal advice *and* on the dance floor. Among her other escorts were Rex Harrison and the actor Robert Hutton.

Lana was also linked with singer Frank Sinatra. He was a married man with children, but Frank cleverly postponed moving his family from New Jersey to Hollywood so he could have his freedom. There were rumors that Lana was the woman responsible for his marital problems, but Frank was on a dating spree and did not want to become involved with any one woman. He did, however, flaunt his affair with Lana by dancing with her all night, meeting her in Palm Springs, and driving around Hollywood with her snuggled up next to him. Columnist Louella Parsons wrote that Lana was only partially responsible for breaking up Sinatra's marriage in 1946. To avoid unfavorable publicity, Lana told Louella she was not in love with Frank and he was not in love with her: "I have never broken up a home."

The Turner-Sinatra relationship was an on-and-off affair for several years, but it was a strictly physical attraction. Frank might have been a skinny, undernourished guy, but he was a fervent and satisfying lover. His second wife, Ava Gardner, said, "It was always great in bed. But the quarreling always started on the way to the bidet." Though Lana was blamed for the initial breakup of Sinatra's marriage, it was his addictive love for Ava that forced him to give up everything: his wife, bank account, and career.

Ava and Lana were both under contract to MGM and very much alike in temperament. Each was divorced from Artie Shaw and had had affairs with Howard Hughes, Robert Taylor, and Clark Gable. Mickey Rooney was involved with Lana and then married to Ava. They were nocturnal creatures, hearty drinkers, heavy smokers, and passionate. To Mayer's frustration, the girls could party all night and report for work looking refreshed and radiant. They knew their lines and were very professional. Ava was a better actress than Lana because she wasn't concerned about her image. She hated Hollywood and the studio system but continued acting because, she said, "I don't know how to do anything else."

The great love of Ava's life was Frank Sinatra, but they couldn't live with each other or without each other. She had many affairs before and after their marriage, but her heart belonged to him and his to her.

In 1945 and 1946 Lana was living life in the fast lane, playing the field. She was having too much fun for thoughts of marriage. Perhaps she toyed with the idea during her romances with Turhan Bey and Howard Hughes, but it's doubtful Lana shed a tear when the affairs ended. Looking back, she knew that youth and innocence were responsible for the Greg Bautzer disaster. On the rebound came Artie Shaw. And if Stephan Crane hadn't fibbed about his credentials, she would have given his marriage proposal more thought.

Lana had learned the hard way and emerged unscathed. Her career was in high gear, she was rich and famous, and she had a beautiful little girl. She had the world at her feet.

Or so she thought.

Chapter 7

✴ TYRONE ✴

THE POSTMAN ALWAYS RINGS TWICE IS ONE of Lana Turner's most memorable films. In 1934 MGM had bought the rights to the daring novel by James M. Cain, the author of *Double Indemnity* and *Mildred Pierce*, but censors banned a film adaptation. Ten years later Metro decided it would be an excellent vehicle for Lana Turner. She hesitated playing the role of a woman who plots her husband's murder, fearing it would blemish her screen image. L. B. Mayer convinced Lana it was time for her to tackle a role that would change her identity, from perennial glamour girl to accomplished actress.

Director Tay Garnett talked to Lana about the proposed script and his idea to dress her in white throughout the picture, creating the illusion of purity. With her platinum hair, Lana was breathtaking and alluring in *Postman* without offending.

One scene stands out: Lana (as Cora), wearing white shorts, high heels, and turban, is standing in the doorway. When her tube of lipstick rolls across the floor, drifter Frank Chambers (played by John Garfield) gazes up at her shapely legs, bare waist, full bosom, and exquisite face. He is surprised to find out she's married to Nick (Cecil Kellaway), the old man who'd hired him to work at their road-side café.

Cora and Frank fall in love. They plan to run away, but she doesn't want to give up her share of the restaurant. It is Cora who comes up with the idea of murdering Nick. After one failed attempt, they succeed and are arrested. A clever lawyer (Hume Cronyn) gets them off with a suspended sentence and advises them to get married to avoid suspicion. When Cora becomes pregnant, she and Frank fall in love all over again and hope to make up for their wrongdoing. On the way home from a midnight swim at the beach, they have a head-on car collision. Cora is killed and Frank is arrested for murder, supposedly to cash in on her insurance policy. He goes to the electric chair, professing his love for Cora.

Lana and John Garfield had a special chemistry on the screen. Director Tay Garnett said, "There was magic between them. I don't know if they had anything going on the side, but sometimes you root for it. John had his fair share of girls, but he had a bad heart and that might have frightened Lana off. John teased her about sex, which tends to make me believe nothing happened. They sizzled on the screen though!"

The Postman Always Rings Twice received rave reviews. The *New York World-Telegram* said, "One of the astonishing excellences of this picture is the performance to which Lana Turner has been inspired." *Life* magazine predicted Lana's all-white wardrobe would become historic. Bosley Crowther of the *New York Times* applauded the picture and wrote that "it gives Lana Turner and John Garfield the best roles of their careers."

"I liked the all-white wardrobe Cora wore and the way

she did her hair," Lana said. "The role gave me something to work with. I understood Cora's yearning for security and respect—yet it led her to do things that ruined her chances of getting what she wanted."

MGM thought Lana should be seen in public with her daughter to offset any bad publicity as a result of *Postman*. Cheryl was photographed with Lana on the movie set and in New York for the premiere. The emphasis was on Lana Turner, model mother. Two-year-old Cheryl had been living a sheltered life at home with a nurse and her grandmother. She was terrified of the crowds screaming "Lana! Lana!" and the hands that reached out for her hair and clothes. Fan magazines wrote about Lana's role as mother and her devotion to Cheryl. All of this was typical of the studio system. If a star's image or reputation was at stake, the children were dragged out of the nursery and dolled up for the press. The youngsters were cuddled by their famous parents (some for the first time), and the older children were told to smile and shut up.

Lana was too busy making films and dating until all hours of the night to spend much time with Cheryl. But while the public lined up to see *The Postman Always Rings Twice*, they were also being introduced to photos and articles of Lana and her adorable little girl.

Keenan Wynn's ex-wife Edie was responsible for Lana's meeting one of the handsomest actors ever to grace the screen, Tyrone Power. The two stars must have been introduced fleetingly at a dinner party or nightclub, but they were under contract to different studios and did not mingle in the same circles. Lana invited Ty home for a drink and their very intense romance began. Not since her affair with

Greg Bautzer had Lana fallen so deeply in love. The problem was that Power was separated from his wife, French actress Annabella, and had not yet filed for divorce.

As usual, Lana threw caution to the wind and became pregnant. She hoped Ty would get a quick divorce and marry her, but when she told him about the baby, he insisted she get an abortion. Terribly hurt and confused, Lana turned to Louis B. Mayer, who arranged for Lana to vacation in South America for two months. Lana made no public appearances in Brazil or Argentina, though an MGM repesentative was always around to handle her flights and accommodations. Whatever publicity Lana received mentioned only her traveling companion, Sara Hamilton.

Tyrone Power was also on a goodwill tour of South America with his friend Cesar Romero and a Fox publicist. If Lana and Ty rendezvoused, it was a well-guarded secret. For Power, it was a last-minute decision, and he flew a twin-motor Beechcraft that provided him with more freedom and privacy than commercial travel.

Before leaving on vacation, Lana told Greg Bautzer to sell her house and find separate residences for herself and Mildred. Lana said, "I'm twenty-six and yet my mother waits up every night until I come home. It's embarrassing to invite a man in for a drink and be greeted by one's mother, who wants to know where I've been and why I came home so late." Bautzer agreed to take care of the details while she was away, but he wasn't happy about being the one to break the news to Mildred. Lana knew that Tyrone was uncomfortable with her mother around. Her plan was to return from South America and begin anew with Tyrone without Mildred's prying eyes. Lana was confident he was going ahead with his divorce and that negotiations were well underway.

* * *

Tyrone Power was born on May 5, 1914, in Cincinnati, Ohio. His father, born and educated in England, was an accomplished stage and screen actor who died in 1932 on the set of *The Miracle Man* in Hollywood. Young Tyrone stayed on to try his luck in films but got only bit parts. He fared better on the Broadway stage under the tutelage of Katharine Cornell. Spotted by a talent scout from 20th Century-Fox, Tyrone took a screen test and was put under contract in 1936. His third film, *Lloyd's of London*, made him a star virtually overnight.

In 1939 Ty married his *Suez* co-star, Annabella, who was five years older, witty, and wise. During an affair with Judy Garland, he enlisted in the Marine Corps and reported for duty in January 1943. Judy was one of many women with whom Power was involved, but when he found out she was pregnant, he came home on leave and asked Annabella for his freedom. She procrastinated until Judy was forced to have an abortion. Ty was devastated to find out because, as he told a friend, "I love Judy so much and I want my baby."

But Power did not stand up to Annabella, whom he would always adore and look to for advice. She accepted his indiscretions and was there for him to lean on during their separations. The marriage, however, was not on solid ground when he was ordered to Saipan in the South Pacific.

In November 1945, Power came home and Annabella was at the pier in Portland to meet him. The romance was out of their marriage, but they supported each other in their careers. She was going to appear on the Broadway stage and he was making *The Razor's Edge* in Hollywood. She consulted him about her play and he consulted her about his contract with 20th Century-Fox. They were apart, but they were very close.

Enter Lana Turner who, coincidentally, followed Judy Garland and Betty Grable in Tyrone Power's life as she did in Artie Shaw's. Betty was admittedly only a playmate, but Lana and Judy seemed to share the disappointment of abortion, as well as the glorious expectation that Ty would marry them. By the time he came home from the South Pacific, however, Judy was Mrs. Vincent Minnelli.

Tyrone Power has often been compared with Robert Taylor, who found it very difficult to "live down" his beautiful face. Both actors were genuinely humble, gentle, loyal to the studio system, and married to older women who were mother substitutes. But Taylor was *not* bisexual or a homosexual.

Power was either or both. He became involved with men originally for the same reason that Clark Gable did: to earn money for a decent meal and to get into films. Gable's was an act of desperation, because he was heterosexual throughout his lifetime.

It didn't occur to Power that he was bisexual until he fell in love with a handsome actor in New York. This did not, however, stop him from proposing marriage to a girlfriend in 1935. Someone said of Power, "He loves men and marries women." But Ty's burden of bisexuality wore heavily on his mind for fear of exposure, which would have ruined his career. He was attracted to both sexes, simple as that. Ty could be faithful to a woman, but eventually the urge to be with a man got the best of him.

Lana moved into a smaller house on Crown Drive in Brentwood with Cheryl, and Mildred settled down in a comfortable apartment. There was decorating to be done in Lana's new home, but she concentrated on Tyrone, who did not respond with her degree of ardor, though he was obviously very much in love. Louis B. Mayer's daughter Edie Goetz said, "Whenever I saw them together, they took my breath away. When they entered a room, everyone was dumbstruck. Lana had platinum hair and Ty's was curly black. I've never seen a more beautiful couple. They talked about doing a film together, but I'm not so sure MGM or Fox would have allowed it. Maybe if Ty had been divorced, but he wasn't, nor was he doing anything about it. He probably might have been husband number three for Lana if he was divorced, but the longer Ty postponed it, the slimmer her chances got."

In late 1946 Lana began filming *Green Dolphin Street,* a costume epic set in the 1840s about two sisters (Lana and Donna Reed) in love with the same man (Richard Hart). He settles in New Zealand and writes home for Donna to join him. In a drunken stupor, he sends for Lana instead. They marry, and she wins his love by enduring the hardships in New Zealand. When Lana discovers it was her sister Hart wanted, she returns home to tell her the truth but finds that Donna has become a nun. The end is bittersweet as Lana and Hart watch Donna take her vows in the Catholic Church.

Tyrone was a frequent visitor to the movie set, and he spent a good deal of time with Lana in her lavish dressing room. She introduced him to the actress who played her maid in the film, Linda Christian, but he paid little notice at the time to the woman who would become his second wife.

Lana knew that 20th Century-Fox was working on a script for Ty titled *Captain from Castile*, a spectacular production that was considered his comeback film following his three years overseas. She was very excited for him but disappointed to find out he would be on location in Mexico over the holidays. Power was elated about the movie and he was relieved to get away from Lana for a while. "She's smothering me," he told a friend.

Edie Goetz confirmed Lana's possessiveness. "But she knew of no other way to love," Edie said. "To her, clinging *was* love, but Ty didn't like it. Lana never said he proposed marriage, but it was taken for granted in Hollywood that they were unofficially engaged."

Fred Lawrence Guiles, author of *Tyrone Power: The Last Idol*, wrote that Lana was on amphetamines that kept her gay most of the time. But often she was clearly out of control. Ty asked her to change doctors, but Lana never got around to it. There were many movie stars who took amphetamines to keep up with their hectic schedules at the studio six days a week. Lana used them to party all night too, and Ty didn't appreciate her extreme mood swings, from giggly gaiety to deep melancholia.

Another problem was Cheryl. Though he loved children, Power did not want her to get used to his company. Lana made sure that many of their weekend outings were a "family" affair, and Ty was becoming very uncomfortable. That he stayed with Lana for almost two years proves that he was trying to make it work. She was, after all, one of the most beautiful, sensitive, and stimulating women he had ever known.

Power left for Patzcuaro, Mexico, in mid-November 1946. Hedda Hopper wrote in her column that he and Lana had "pledged their love" to one another. Hedda asked Ty outright if he was in love with Lana. He replied, "Well, it's the nearest I've ever come to it." Always the gentleman, he told Hedda that people had the wrong impression of Lana: that she'd led a difficult life and been hurt because she trusted people.

Lana, in turn, said that Tyrone was the first man who thought of her as more than just a pretty face and that he was sincerely interested in her feelings.

Power flew to Mexico for at least three months to film *Captain of Castile*. Meanwhile, Lana was working hard on *Green Dolphin Street*. But shortly after Christmas, she couldn't take being separated from Ty much longer. In their last phone conversation, he said filming had been delayed by bad weather. With the horrible thought that they would be apart longer than expected, Lana suddenly decided to fly to Mexico City. She had three days off for New Year's, giving her plenty of time to be with Tyrone and report back to work.

But when Lana arrived in Mexico City, she found out there were no buses or trains to Patzcuaro, about a hundred miles away. Told that the roads were bad, Lana went into a panic and called Tyrone. "I planned to surprise you," she said, "so we could have a belated Christmas dinner together."

"How's the weather in Los Angeles?" he asked.

"Darling, I'm in Mexico City!"

"Christ! What the hell are you doing in Mexico City?"

"I want to toast the New Year with you."

Ty uttered a few curse words under his breath and tried to be civil. "You stay put and I'll try to find a plane," he said.

Lana could tell by the sound of his voice that her visit

was not a pleasant surprise. Ty was clearly annoyed, but when he met her at the small airport near Patzcuaro, he appeared to have had a change of heart. Lana described their very romantic New Year's Eve together in her memoirs: the jewels she wore in her hair, the church bells ringing, people dancing and singing in the streets, sweet wine and kisses. They glanced into one another's eyes with thoughts that "this is forever." It was the most beautiful night of her life.

News of Lana's trip reached Los Angeles. Louis B. Mayer was furious. "Does she have to chase a man all the way to Mexico?" he asked Howard Strickling. "Doesn't she have enough action in this town?"

Reporters called Mrs. Power in New York with the news that her husband had spent the weekend in Mexico with Lana Turner. Annabella scolded the press for disturbing her with such trivia.

Lana's plans to return to Los Angeles on Monday, January 6, 1947, backfired. Heavy rains washed out the roads to Mexico City and planes were unable to take off. Her tears of happiness turned to tears of frustration. "I wept for two days," she said, knowing that it would cost MGM a fortune in production delays on *Green Dolphin Street*.

Power was disturbed too, but there was nothing anyone could do until the heavy rains stopped. When the weather cleared and Lana was about to depart, she told him, "I'll be back, darling, but next time I won't have to rush."

Lana expected problems with Mayer when she returned, but it was worse than expected. The movie set was dark. She was about to burst into tears when the lights came on and everyone on the set, wearing serapes and sombreros, began to sing "South of the Border." Thanks to the director, Victor Saville, who'd shot around her to avoid shutting down, Lana was spared. Mayer could have suspended her—fired her, in fact—for not reporting on schedule, but it would have been MGM's loss.

Annabella, in France to film *The Eternal Conflict*, told the press she had no intention of proceeding with a divorce from Ty. To clear up the matter of her being blamed for standing in his way of marrying Lana, she said, "The truth is I had to ask Ty to get a lawyer as I have done—to arrange our divorce." Annabella might have sued him, but Ty asked her not to put him in a vulnerable position with Lana.

Power returned to Hollywood for interior filming of *Captain from Castille* on January 31, 1946. Within days, he and Lana were seen together everywhere, closer than before. When she approached the subject of marriage, Ty said there was nothing he could do about it until Annabella finished her movie and came home. Lana bought his excuse, and just as well, because Power wanted their relationship to continue with no strings attached. That he was faithful to her—and she to him—was good enough for now.

While Lana was filming *Cass Timberlane* with Spencer Tracy, Ty was on the movie set every day. He was at odds with his boss, Darryl Zanuck, over *Nightmare Alley*, a film about a phony psychic reduced to working as a geek in a cheap carnival. Lana's support gave Ty the encouragement he needed to fight for the role that was so unlike any he had ever tackled. Until he could convince 20th Century-Fox, Ty spent his time with Lana at MGM.

Cass Timberlane, based on Sinclair Lewis's novel, is set in a small town, with Spencer Tracy in the title role of a middle-aged judge who marries a young girl (Lana) from the wrong side of the tracks. She has problems adjusting to his stuffy friends and the loss of their baby. During their separation, she is seriously injured in an auto accident, and her husband rushes to her bedside for a reconciliation.

Cass Timberlane was considered a fine movie for two reasons: Spencer Tracy and Lana Turner. Critics thought he was perfect as the patient and understanding judge. And Lana was right for the flighty but sweet young wife who loves him deeply. *Variety* said she was the surprise of the picture with her fine performance. The *Daily News* wrote that "Turner is able to hold the spotlight while Spencer Tracy is on the scene," saying it was due to "her ability as an actress and a charmer."

Lana has always been gorgeous on the screen, but she had a special glow in *Cass Timberlane,* blossoming with love for Tyrone Power. His presence on the set was an added incentive.

In May, Power began *Nightmare Alley.* He did a superb job, but Zanuck rushed it into neighborhood theaters in October before releasing the stupendous *Captain of Castile* two months later. *Nightmare Alley,* in black and white, became a cult film after Power's death. Zanuck got the response he wanted from *Captain of Castile,* in which Power is handsome and dashing in vivid Technicolor alongside Jean Peters, the future Mrs. Howard Hughes.

MGM released *Green Dolphin Street* and *Cass Timberlane* in October 1947, and they were both moneymakers. It had been a hectic few months for Lana and Ty.

She hoped they could sneak off together to some remote place, but before she had a chance to discuss it, Power announced he was going on another goodwill tour, this time to Africa. Lana wasn't invited along, of course, but she was determined to announce their engagement before Ty's departure.

Chapter 8

✳ REBOUND ✳

*L*ANA GAVE A LAVISH FAREWELL PARTY for Ty, who was not aware that she had chosen the Cupid theme. Love, love, love, with the letters L and T entwined with an arrow. He was visibly uncomfortable as guests waited for the couple to name the day. Lana hoped Ty would be influenced by the romantic setting and give in, but he couldn't wait to get out.

Still in there plugging, Lana was at the airport on September 1 to see Power off. She told reporters, "I'll meet him in Africa when my picture is finished." Ty was agreeable to the rendezvous, but it was a relief to get away from her. Obviously mixed up, he told one friend the romance was over. To another he said, "I need time. It might work out."

From here on, there are several versions as to what happened. Did Lana resume an affair with Frank Sinatra to make Ty jealous? Or did a girlfriend betray Lana by telling Power about her dates with Frank? Or did Ty read about it in the newspaper and use Lana's unfaithfulness as an excuse to end the affair?

It's possible that Power heard rumors about Sinatra's dates with Lana in New York. She admitted to having dinner with Frank but insisted they were only good friends. After all, she had flown east on her first leg to meeting Ty abroad. Then quite suddenly Lana couldn't reach him. He had decided to stop off in Rome for a few days and was staying at the Excelsior Hotel. Also registered there was actress Linda Christian, who had played Lana's maid in *Green Dolphin Street*. Linda called Ty about her little sister's mad crush on him and asked if they could get together. Ty and Linda fell in love during his two-week stay in Rome. Hollywood columnists later speculated that he was so hurt over Lana's unfaithfulness, he was fair game. This is unlikely, because Power was a married man and had too much to lose. Edie Goetz said, "Ty was concerned all along that Lana could not be satisfied with one man. She might have been more discreet about her dates with Sinatra because she'd been linked with him before. If Ty used this as an excuse to break up with Lana, he didn't have to marry another woman."

Power managed to avoid Lana's calls to Rome. When she finally got him on the phone, Linda Christian was in his room. Lana was upset and began yelling at Ty, who said very little. "Say you love me!" she shouted. "Tell me right now!"

"I love you," he managed.

Before Ty hung up the phone, he halfheartedly told Lana he would meet her in New York. Instead, he landed in Kansas City before going on to California on November 25. He called Lana, who was waiting for him in New York.

"What happened?" she asked.

"I had to get back."

"I'll be on the next plane to Los Angeles," she said. "You'll pick me up at the airport?"

"Yes . . . if that's what you want . . ."

But when Lana arrived, Ty wasn't there yet. She waited quite a while for him to show up, and they barely spoke to each other on the way home. While he made cocktails, Lana was sure something was terribly wrong and she asked him if there was another woman. Power replied, "Yes, there is."

"I wish you'd leave," she said, holding back the tears.

He paused for a moment, gulped down his highball, and walked to the door. Before leaving, Power turned to Lana and said, "I hope we can be friends."

"Get out!" she hissed.

The minute the door closed, Lana ran upstairs, threw herself on the bed, and wept.

Meanwhile Annabella flew into Los Angeles and told reporters she was prepared to divorce Power if he wanted to remarry. This was undoubtedly her way of getting even with Lana, because Ty did not know anything about his wife's statement to the press until it was too late.

MGM and 20th Century-Fox were forced to intervene. Darryl Zanuck suggested Tyrone use the patriotic approach. The House Un-American Activities Committee was investigating the infiltration of Communism in Hollywood, and big stars were volunteering to testify. Thus Power told the press he was glad to be back home "in a democracy" after seeing how Communism was spreading throughout Europe and elsewhere. "I want to do my part," he said.

Mayer advised Lana to follow up on this. She told Hedda Hopper, "Ty came back from Europe determined to fight Communism, which he believes, as we all do, is the scourge of the world. So we decided to go our separate ways. We never discussed marriage, but the press did and that put us in an awkward position. From now on I will carry my chin a little higher and work harder."

On January 26, 1948, Annabella was granted a divorce from Power, who paid dearly for his freedom to marry the woman he loved—Linda Christian.

Lana was shattered. After Power's death in 1958, Lana confessed that Ty was the love of her life. "He was the one who broke my heart," she said.

Tyrone Power married Linda Christian in Rome on January 27, 1949. "Gee," he said, "I never dreamed of having a wife so brilliant she can speak seven languages." They had two daughters, Romina (1951) and Taryn (1953). But Tyrone's dedication to his work, Linda's determination to resume her film career, and frequent separations put a severe strain on their marriage. He had numerous lovers of both sexes, and Linda began a not-so-secret affair with the actor Edmund Purdom. In May 1955, she filed for divorce.

Ty said he would never marry again. However, a pretty twenty-six-year-old Southern girl named Debbie Minardos changed his mind, and on May 7, 1958, they were married in Tunica, Mississippi. Six weeks later, Ty announced that his wife was pregnant and he was hoping for a son. But on November 15, Power had a fatal heart attack on the set of *Solomon and Sheba*. He was forty-four years old.

His son, Tyrone, was born on January 22, 1959.

While Lana was pursuing Tyrone in 1947 she made *Homecoming*, a World War II film directed by Mervyn LeRoy. It is the tragic love story of a married Army doctor (Clark Gable) and his nurse, "Snapshot," played by Lana. To avoid getting involved with him, she asks for a transfer, but they meet again and consummate their love. A short time later she is wounded and dies with him at her bedside.

Homecoming had less impact than Lana's other two films with Gable. Bosley Crowther of the *New York Times* wrote, "It is really nothing more than a cheap, synthetic chunk of romance designed to exploit two gaudy stars." The New York *Daily News* said, "Gable and Turner are Gable and Turner, and that's all their fans want."

Regrettably, Lana was not given credit for a fine performance as Snapshot. Perhaps moviegoers (and critics) were annoyed at having to sit for over an hour before experiencing the thrill of a Turner-Gable kiss.

When Lana finished *Homecoming* she rushed to New York, on her way, or so she thought, to meet Tyrone. The results were almost as pathetic as her on-screen romance with Gable.

Lana was besieged by the press when news of her split with Ty was made public. Adding to her misery was an audit by the Internal Revenue Service. She turned this matter over to her accountants and fled to New York with Cheryl and Mildred in early December 1947, a week after the Power romance ended.

Lana had never been so vulnerable. Still in love with Power, she was ready for a good time in New York. When she received a call from an avid admirer, Bob Topping, she almost turned him down again. He had sent her flowers and candy at the studio, but Lana ignored his calls. When Topping got through to her at the Plaza Hotel, she wanted to know if he was still married to the actress Arline Judge. He assured her they were legally separated, so Lana agreed to go out with him. Besides, she needed a date for a premiere.

The slightly overweight, balding, thirty-three-year-old millionaire wasn't Lana's type, but he had social standing and a charm all his own. He also had a pair of Cartier diamond earrings for her that evening. Lana declined, but Topping insisted she wear them as a favor to him.

Henry J. Topping, known in social circles as "Bob," and his brothers, Dan (former owner of the New York Yankees) and Jack, were tin-plate heirs whose $140 million fortune had been amassed by their maternal grandfather, Daniel J. Reid. Dan's ex-wives were skating star Sonja Henie and Arline Judge, who became his sister-in-law when she became Bob's third wife in May 1947. From his second marriage to the half-sister of George and Alfred Gwynne Vanderbilt, Bob had two children, Sandra and Henry, Jr.

Lana knew precisely who Bob Topping was and how much he was worth. Friends had tried to convince her to go out with him earlier because he was such a "good catch," but she'd had eyes only for Tyrone.

On December 10, 1947, Lana found out what it was like to be on a blind date with a millionaire playboy whose roots were *not* in Hollywood. They slipped out of the Astor theater without being noticed and went to a posh Park Avenue party. Society hostess Elsa Maxwell greeted them fondly. Lana slipped out of her fur coat and whispered to Elsa, "Where do I check this thing?"

"My God, Lana, this isn't a nightclub!" With that, a butler with a scowling face gently took her coat.

The crème de la crème were there, and although they were interested in seeing Lana Turner in person, the socialites were far more elegant in their finest from Bergdorf's and Saks. Elsa told Lana discreetly, "You'll have to adjust to Park Avenue because Park Avenue will never lower itself to Hollywood."

Lana wasn't the least bit impressed by the best-dressed ladies of the Social Register or with the Duchess of Windsor. "I think they're all a bit stuffy and dull," she said.

"But very, very rich," Elsa reminded her. "And very, very influential."

"Maybe," Lana retorted, "but no one I've ever met has more power than Louis B. Mayer, and that includes the president of the United States."

After several more dates with Topping, Lana accepted his invitation to spend the Christmas holidays at his mansion in Connecticut. "My family and your family," he said. She accepted without hesitation.

Topping's Round Hill estate in Greenwich, Connecticut, was awesome even for a movie star who had grown accustomed to the tinsel and glamour of Hollywood. The Tudor-style brick mansion, situated on six hundred acres, had forty-three rooms, marble fireplaces, maids, butlers, and cooks. Inside the beautifully landscaped gardens were tennis courts and a swimming pool.

It was the perfect holiday for Lana and Cheryl, who had never seen a white Christmas. There was such a heavy snowstorm that Bob's plans for a New Year's Eve party were canceled. He wasn't disappointed, however, because this meant he had more time to discuss marriage with Lana. She was honest about not loving him, but the millionaire predicted, "You will."

Before returning to Hollywood, Lana dined with Bob at the "21" club in New York. Sipping a dry martini, she suddenly caught sight of something sparkling in her cocktail glass. "What is it?" she asked.

"Why don't you find out?" he said with a wink.

Lana dipped her finger into the martini and there, in all its splendor, was a fifteen-carat marquise diamond ring. "What's it for?" she gasped.

"I'm asking you to marry me, Lana. Will you?"

"Yes." She sighed, putting the rock on her engagement finger.

Lana said it might have been the martinis or the biggest diamond she had ever seen that convinced her to marry Topping. But there were two other very good reasons. She wanted to show Tyrone she wasn't pining away for him. And she needed Bob's financial backing in case MGM suspended her without pay for turning down *The Three Musketeers*.

Louis B. Mayer was appalled by Lana's outrageous behavior in recent months. Columnists hinted that she had broken up Frank Sinatra's marriage, but she went out with him anyway, ignoring repeated warnings from MGM. Then she had become "engaged" to Tyrone Power, who also had a wife. Just prior to meeting Topping, Lana had had a brief but public encounter in New York with John Alden Talbot, Jr., a good-looking tycoon. Mrs. Talbot named Lana as corespondent in her January 1948 divorce suit.

MGM was prepared to suspend Lana for misconduct before her affair with Topping became front-page news. When his wife, Arline Judge, claimed her marriage to Bob had been just fine until Miss Turner came along, Mayer cringed.

On January 10, 1948, Lana, wearing her fifteen-carat engagement ring, arrived back in Hollywood with Topping. On the fourteenth, MGM suspended her without pay for having been five days late in reporting to work and then turning down the part of Lady de Winter in *The Three Musketeers*. Mayer told Lana that she would be responsible for preproduction costs, which might run into several hundred thousand dollars. She complained that the part of Lady de Winter was too small, but if he'd build it up she'd honor her commitment. He agreed to have the script revised, and a week after her suspension, Lana was put back on salary at $5,000 a week. She told columnist Louella Parsons, "I could never disappoint Louis B. Mayer. He's been too good to me."

Everybody concerned was a winner. MGM needed Lana's name on the marquee, and she was exquisite in her first technicolor film with an all-star cast: Gene Kelly as D'Artagnan; Van Heflin, Gig Young, and Robert Coote as the three musketeers; June Allyson as Lady Constance; and Vincent Price as Richelieu. Lana was the villainess, Lady de Winter, who schemes, seduces, and murders to dethrone King Louis XIII. At the end, she is beheaded for her crimes.

The *New York Times*'s Bosley Crowther called *The Three Musketeers* a "splendiferous" production, adding that "more dazzling costumes, more colors or more of Miss Turner's chest have never been seen in a picture like this one."

Lana enjoyed making the picture, despite her reluctance at the onset. MGM proudly promoted *Musketeers* in bold letters: LANA TURNER! FIRST TIME IN TECHNICOLOR! The film was a big success in 1948, but is not one of Lana's most memorable pictures.

Bob Topping rented a house in Beverly Hills and sued Arline Judge for divorce. He wanted to marry Lana before she changed her mind, but when Arline failed to cooperate, MGM demanded that Lana deny her plans to marry Topping and to avoid reporters and columnists. But in April, Arline agreed to a settlement of $500,000 after testifying that Bob had physically abused her repeatedly during their brief marriage. The divorce was granted in Bridgeport,

Connecticut, on Friday, April 23. Lana immediately announced that she would marry Topping on the following Monday at Billy Wilkerson's mansion on Sunset Boulevard.

Lana was determined to have a proper wedding with all the trimmings after eloping twice. Her wedding gown of champagne-colored Alençon lace over champagne satin was designed by Don Loper.

She asked that Billy's house be filled with hundreds of flowers, roses, gladioli, and daisies. The altar was a mass of five thousand gardenias, and the bride carried a cluster of magnificent orchids, flown in from Hawaii. Louis B. Mayer, Greg Bautzer, Joan Crawford, and Louella Parsons were among the sixty-five invited guests who feasted on a lavish buffet surrounded by lakes and rivers in which live goldfish swam.

Following the two-o'clock ceremony, the bride and groom kissed. He said in a loud whisper, "This is forever." She smiled sweetly and replied, "Yes, darling," gazing down at the magnificent two-inch-wide diamond bracelet that Bob had given to her for a wedding present.

Though Lana said she'd wanted a dignified wedding, there was little she could do to prevent MGM press agents and seventy-five reporters from attending a champagne reception after the regular guests had departed. This was the price she paid for being a movie goddess and allowing MGM to share the expenses. So Lana's dignified wedding turned into a sideshow and was reported as such. "Lana Turner's Fourth" was the theme, and columnists poked fun at a ham decorated with "I love you" and a roast beef adorned with "She loves him."

Life magazine featured a very unflattering article about the Topping wedding. It said Lana wore heavy pancake makeup, the color of her dress was unbecoming, and she was so nervous that the bouquet of white orchids trembled "as if they were in a storm. In a way they were."

The Toppings spent their wedding night at the Beverly Hills Hotel. A late breakfast was set up on the front porch of their private cottage the next morning, but columnist Hedda Hopper was eating it when the couple emerged. Lana had to control her temper, because Hedda and Louella Parsons could make or break a star. Topping fumed as the columnist rattled off stupid questions, such as "Do you love each other?" and "Will this marriage last, Lana, or are you on the rebound?"

On May 5, the newlyweds sailed on the *Mauretania* to Europe on their honeymoon, but not before they were beseiged by fans and newsmen at the pier and aboard ship. Representatives from MGM were not on hand to protect Lana from the mobs and reporters; most likely she didn't want them there as a favor to Bob, who was fed up with the enormous publicity and lack of privacy. The mad crush at the New York sailing was only the beginning of a disastrous honeymoon.

The British, who had not recovered from the ravages of World War II, were not impressed with Lana's extravagance. She had so many pieces of luggage, the number of trunks and suitcases wasn't specified, just photographed. Lana failed to endear herself to the British newsmen, who referred to her as "rude and plump," and she managed to be late for every press conference. The London papers concentrated on Lana's marriages and her latest husband, the millionaire, who never smiled. American newsmen, meanwhile, were writing that the Presbyterian minister who'd presided at the wedding ceremony had done so illegally, since Church doctrine stated he could not marry anyone who was not divorced for one year, and the groom had been single for less than three days. Eventually this was resolved because the Reverend MacLennan was retired. When news of this reached the British, they threw rocks at Lana's limousine and hissed when they saw the Toppings on the street.

Bob wanted to combine business with pleasure to pay for the honeymoon, but his midget auto-racing business in England was a flop, to the tune of almost half a million dollars. Topping could well afford the loss, but it was one of his financial ventures that he particularly enjoyed. Lana said their stay in London was a terrible disappointment, but Paris and the French Riviera made up for the annoying first half of their honeymoon. She and Bob mingled with the yacht set in Cannes, entertaining on their own chartered boat and being wined and dined by the elite. "It was glorious," Lana said.

In September they returned to Round Hill in Connecticut. When Lana became pregnant, she hinted at the possibility of giving up her career. Bob didn't want her to work anyway. He enjoyed the good life in the East and didn't want Lana obligated to MGM. That he was willing to buy up her contract gave Lana more power over the studio. Journalist Adela Rogers St. Johns concluded that most actresses talk about retiring because they get exhausted and can't find a place to hide. St. Johns predicted Lana was too involved in her work and the limelight to give them up.

But for now, Topping had Lana all to himself while she waited for the baby. There were parties going on constantly at Round Hill, and Bob was drinking very heavily. Lana knew he liked his liquor and she drank more than usual with him, but now it was getting out of hand. Guests frequently stayed overnight, and late the next morning, Bloody Marys were served to cure hangovers. Then the party started all over again. On weekends, it wasn't unusual for a hundred people to attend a party at Round Hill.

If Lana was disturbed by her husband's excessive drinking, there were compensations. The Topping brothers divided the valuable jewelry that their mother had left to them, and Lana became the proud owner of a priceless emerald ring and pearls of the finest quality. Anyone who knew Lana well could verify that she was obsessed with fine jewelry.

Christmas at Round Hill was another fantasy experience, and on New Year's Eve, a live band played dance music for sixty couples in formal attire. But Lana's life was never blissful for long. In January 1949, she went into premature labor and was rushed to Doctors Hospital in New York. The Rh factor was responsible for the stillbirth of a son when Lana was six months pregnant.

When she felt stronger, Bob wanted to go on an extended vacation in the Caribbean on his yacht. They spent a leisurely few months sailing, fishing, swimming, and socializing. This was one of the happiest times of Lana's life, but it turned out to be the pinnacle of her marriage to Topping.

MGM wanted Lana back in Hollywood for *A Life of Her Own* in the summer of 1949. She joked about her clothes being too tight from all the gourmet dinners and constant drinking. As the time drew near for her to face the cameras, she weighed herself and was shocked to find out she had gained over thirty pounds. A doctor put her on a very strict diet, which made Lana nervous and abrupt. Bob was not in a good mood either, when he found out he couldn't afford the maintainance and taxes on Round Hill. When it was put up for sale, he and Lana decided to settle in California. While she counted calories and he counted his financial losses, their marriage was deteriorating.

Lana's home on Crown Street was too small, so they moved into a twenty-four-room, two-story Georgian-style house in Holmby Hills on Mapleton Drive with her money. Bob was trying to recoup his losses by investing what capital he had left. Yet he continued to buy Lana expensive diamonds and furs. Perhaps the luxurious gifts helped to keep the marriage together, just as the fifteen-carat diamond ring had convinced Lana to marry Topping in the first place. By the early months on 1949 Lana had begun to fall in love with Bob, but it was too late. She realized he was an alcoholic, and his heavy financial losses meant she would have to be the breadwinner in the family.

Lana went back to work in *A Life of Her Own*. She played a small-town girl who goes to New York, becomes a top model, and falls in love with a married man (Ray Milland). Lana visits his wife to plead for a divorce. The woman is crippled and obviously very dependent on her husband, so Lana breaks off the affair and begins a new life.

A Life of Her Own got bad reviews. Bosley Crowther of the *New York Times* agreed with the other critics: "Two years' absence from the movies obviously did not improve Lana Turner's talents as an actress or her studio's regard for what she can do."

Crowther was right about MGM. Louis B. Mayer was busy with his racehorses and his courtship of a young new wife. He hired Dore Schary as production head in 1948, hoping to put MGM in the black again after a $6.5 million

TOP TO BOTTOM: Hedy Lamarr, Lana Turner, and Judy Garland in *Ziegfeld Girl* (1941). The film marked a major turning point in Lana's movie career. *(Archive Photos)*

LEFT: Clark Gable and Lana Turner in *Honky Tonk* (1941). Gable's jealous wife, Carole Lombard, was not allowed on the movie set. *(Archive Photos)*

BELOW: Lana Turner in the unforgettable *The Postman Always Rings Twice* (1946). *(Archive Photos)*

Lana with her first
husband, bandleader
Artie Shaw.
(*Archive Photos*)

Husband number two,
Stephen Crane, and Lana,
holding their daughter
Cheryl in 1943.
(*Archive Photos*)

ABOVE: Actor Tyrone
Power was the love of
Lana's life, but he got
away. (*Archive Photos*)

RIGHT: Lana married
millionaire Bob Topping
in 1948 on the rebound
after Tyrone Power left
her. (*Archive Photos*)

TOP LEFT: Actor Lex Barker, husband number four, was thrown out of the house after Lana accused him of abusing her daughter Cheryl. (*Archive Photos*)

BOTTOM LEFT: Lana and her fifth husband, Fred May. (*Archive Photos*)

BOTTOM RIGHT: Why Lana married her seventh husband, Ronald Dante remains a mystery. It was a disaster. (*Archive Photos*)

ABOVE: Lana talking
to her daughter Cheryl
in her attorney's office
where depositions were
taken.
(*Archive Photos*)

RIGHT: Lana Turner
gives the performance
of her life to prove
that Cheryl killed
gangster Johnny
Stompanato in self-
defense.
(*Archive Photos*)

ABOVE: Cheryl, Lana, Josh, and Mildred.
(*The Collection of Taylor Pero*)

LEFT: A candid photograph taken by Lana's secretary-companion, Taylor Pero.
(*The Collection of Taylor Pero*)

Lana and her daughter, Cheryl. *(Archive Photos)*

deficit. But Mayer was gradually losing control of his beloved studio, and he was forced to resign in June 1951. His stars were not particularly fond of Schary or his projects. Lana had to deal with him for the first time during *A Life of Her Own*. Originally Wendell Corey was her leading man in the film, and although Lana didn't feel he was right for the part of her rich lover, Schary refused to listen. Not long after production began, Lana was late on the set because her dress didn't fit. Corey remarked, "The wonderful Barbara Stanwyck never keeps us waiting." Lana knew he was referring to the Robert Taylor affair, and she refused to work until Corey was replaced by Ray Milland.

Schary infuriated Lana once again by putting her into the forgettable *Mr. Imperium* with Ezio Pinza, who had just finished a run on the Broadway stage in *South Pacific*. Lana pleaded for another picture, but she was forced into a silly plot about a European prince who falls in love with an American nightclub singer. Lana disliked Pinza, whom she described as a conceited womanizer with bad breath.

Mr. Imperium was so bad, Radio City Music Hall canceled the booking. *Photoplay* magazine said, "The story never jells." The *New York Times* thought Lana and her wardrobe were beautiful, but "it is hardly likely that anyone would envy her dialogue."

Pinza's career in Hollywood ended after one more picture. Lana survived, of course. No matter how bad the movie was, her beautiful face and figure were never disappointing.

On May 24, 1950, Lana placed her hands and feet in wet cement on the sidewalk entrance of Grauman's Chinese Theater on Hollywood Boulevard. After she had signed her name, the crowd clamored for the Sweater Girl to leave behind another imprint. Lana shook her head and smiled. "This is really an honor," she said breathlessly.

And indeed it was. Thousands made good in Hollywood, but only 170 stars are forever immortalized at Grauman's.

Chapter 9

✳ OH, NO! NOT AGAIN! ✳

$\mathcal{I}$N OCTOBER 1950, LANA HAD ANOTHER miscarriage due to the Rh factor. She desperately wanted this baby, because Bob seemed to be slipping away into his own world of booze and gambling. Sober, he was a lamb. After one drink he was mellow. Then his Mr. Hyde emerged. Bob never hit Lana, but he smashed dishes, lamps, and whatever else was within reach during his arguments with her. The next day he apologized for outbursts he couldn't remember.

Mildred didn't want to worry Lana after the miscarriage, but the time had come for someone to check over the bills that were piling up. Lana blamed herself for some of the ones stamped overdue, but Bob was responsible for the majority of them.

"I can't believe it," she exclaimed.

"Face it," Mildred said. "You can't afford to support a millionaire."

Lana threw up her arms and sighed. She wanted the marriage to survive, but Bob's solution to any problem was "Let's have a drink." Lana tried to keep up with him in the evenings, but her weight was a problem and she knew it was caused by too much liquor. Without a drinking companion at home, Bob went out at night. His pattern of disappearing made Lana suspicious, so she had him followed and found out he was seeing other women. When Lana confronted Bob, he packed his bags and left home. She heard from friends that he'd gone fishing in Oregon. Some time later, Lana got word that Bob was in New York, consulting his attorneys about a separation.

"Oh, no. Not again!" she cried.

On September 11, 1951, MGM announced that Lana was divorcing Bob Topping "because he insisted she give up her career." Hollywood insiders knew that he was hiding out in Sun Valley with Mona Moedl, an ice-skating instructor.

Maybe Lana could have faced another divorce gracefully if she and Bob had talked it over and decided they were at an impasse. But knowing he was involved with someone else was the crowning blow after two disastrous movies, and now L. B. Mayer was no longer there to watch over her at MGM. Lana wondered if there was anything worth living for. She had been so busy with her marriages and career that Cheryl was closer to her father and grandmother. Lonely and depressed, Lana had a few drinks and decided to take her own life. She took some sleeping pills and slashed her wrist with a razor. Mildred found her in a pool of blood in the bathroom and called their doctor, who rushed Lana to Hollywood Presbyterian Hospital.

Cheryl said she was told the following day that her mother felt faint in the shower and accidentally cut her wrist when she fell through the glass door. (Cheryl went directly to the bathroom and found the glass door intact.) That was the explanation MGM gave to the press when news leaked out that Lana's wrist was stitched and bandaged in the hospital. News photographers wanted a picture of the Turner bathroom the next morning, but Lana's agent, Ben Cole, said the shattered glass had been replaced. If the "accident" had occurred around two o'clock in the morning, reporters didn't believe the door could possibly be replaced so quickly.

Lana began to wear more bracelets than usual to cover up the fine scar that was proof her wrist wasn't cut by jagged glass. Was the suicide attempt a cry for help? In her memoirs Lana said she wanted to die, but she didn't cut deep enough or take a lethal dose of sleeping pills. According to one of her secretaries, Lana had made a vain attempt at killing herself again, and she was not in danger.

Lana did not start divorce proceedings until the fall of 1952. She claimed the negotiations were long and tedious, but there are theories that Lana was holding out for a big sum of money or hoping Bob would come back. She finally settled for $225,000. Topping, however, wanted either her house in California or his mother's heirloom jewelry returned. Trying to get Lana to part with diamonds and pearls wasn't easy, but saving her house was worth the sacrifice.

Lana got to keep all of the other magnificent jewelry that Bob had given her during their marriage, which had lasted three and a half years. She said the Topping fortune had dwindled drastically after Sonja Henie divorced Dan in 1946.

When Bob was free he married Mona Moedl in 1953. He died fifteen years later, at the age of fifty-four.

Shortly after her suicide attempt, Lana started filming a remake of *The Merry Widow* in Technicolor. In the title role of the beautiful and rich widow, she is sought after for her money by a handsome count, played by Fernando

Lamas. Before he has a chance to meet her, she poses as a struggling chorus girl to throw him off. He falls in love with the "poor" girl before she reveals her identity. At the end they dance to the strings of "The Merry Widow Waltz."

Lana either wore gloves and wide bracelets or carried a fur in the picture to conceal her bandaged wrist. But her depression and feelings of hopelessness faded away in the arms of her leading man after working hours. For a woman who had no reason for living only a few days earlier, Lana was absolutely radiant in *The Merry Widow*. Why? Because she was madly in love with the Argentine actor.

Fernando Lamas, who signed a contract with MGM in 1950, was dubbed the Latin Lover. His first starring role was in *The Merry Widow*, and he displayed a very effective baritone singing voice. Lamas, thirty-six, was separated from his second wife, but he had no intention of getting a divorce. Lana was in the same situation with Bob Topping, but her romance with Lamas was so highly publicized she felt somewhat embarrassed when he told the press in her company that he was not seeking a divorce. Fernando liked the attention he was getting in the Hollywood columns as Lana Turner's boyfriend, and MGM took advantage of it. They were quite an item for about a year. Fernando's wife eventually divorced him, but he humiliated Lana once more by stating publicly, "I have no intention of getting married again." What gossip columnists did not print was that he had keys to Lana's house, coming and going as he pleased. Neither dated anyone else à la the Tyrone Power fiasco, but Lana was sure Lamas would be her next husband.

Before establishing residence in Reno to finalize her divorce from Topping, Lana made one of her most memorable movies: *The Bad and the Beautiful*, with Kirk Douglas, who played the "bad" movie mogul to Lana's "beautiful" drunken actress. Douglas takes a chance on Lana and transforms her into a great star. He allows her to love him until she has all of Hollywood at her feet. When she finds him with another woman at his home, Lana runs out the front door in tears, gets into her car, and drives into the blaring headlights of oncoming cars in a heavy rainstorm. The viewer gets the impression she will be killed in a head-on collision. Instead, her car goes off the road into a ditch, and Lana weeps uncontrollably, slumped over the steering wheel. This is her biggest scene in the picture, and Lana handled it admirably.

The *New York Times*'s Bosley Crowther, who usually praised Lana, said, "She is an actress playing an actress and neither one is real. A howling act in a wildly racing auto—pure bunk—is the top of her speed." In contrast, *Film Quarterly* magazine thought the scene was "one of the most exciting sequences of the decade for a picture."

The Bad and the Beautiful won five Oscars in 1952: for best supporting actress (Gloria Grahame), screenplay (Charles Schnee), cinematography, art direction/set decoration, and costume design.

Kirk Douglas, who was nominated for best actor, but lost to Gary Cooper for *High Noon*, said the papers predicted a hot romance between him and Lana. "I was ready for it," he said. "But she was going with Fernando Lamas, who was terribly jealous. He was always around, so nothing happened."

But the rumors of an affair between Lana and Kirk persisted. She called Louella Parsons to protest. "I have never seen Kirk off the set," Lana insisted, "but the items keep appearing. I'm in love with Fernando Lamas, and no other man means a thing to me."

MGM announced that Lana would co-star again with Lamas in *Latin Lovers*. But shortly before production began, they attended a party at Marion Davies's fabulous beach house in Malibu. During the evening Lex Barker, of *Tarzan* fame, asked Lana to dance. Fernando seethed when she accepted and flirted openly with Lex on the dance floor. They returned to the table and Lamas shouted at Barker, "Why don't you take her out in the bushes and fuck her?"

The other guests expected a fistfight and froze, with all eyes on Lana, who bid a swift goodnight to friends. Lamas took her home where a bitter battle ensued—a battle that Lana refused to describe in her autobiography. A week later the bruises and scratches were still visible, but Lana had to report for *Latin Lovers*. Rather than talk to Dore Schary, she went to an old friend, Benny Thau, head of MGM talent. Benny was appalled by the black-and-blue marks on Lana's body. She told him the truth, and Benny said he would see to it that Lamas was replaced in *Latin Lovers*.

Ricardo Montalban was born in Mexico and has often been compared to Lamas, who had more sex appeal, but Montalban was an able substitute though his voice was dubbed.

In *Latin Lovers* Lana is cast again as a very rich woman who is never sure if men are attracted to her or her money. When she meets Montalban, a plantation owner, in Brazil they fall in love. Lana realizes this is the real thing and does a turnabout by giving him the headaches of her fortune when they marry.

Crowther of the *New York Times* apparently preferred Lana in Technicolor. He thought she was terrible in *The Bad and the Beautiful*, done in black and white, but he said she was lovelier than ever in *Latin Lovers* and praised her magnificent wardrobe. Crowther also raved about Lana's dancing the samba with Montalban: "a talent that should not go unnoticed."

Though Benny Thau assured Lana she would not be harassed by Fernando Lamas, she wanted to get out of town after *Latin Lovers* was finished. Frank Sinatra, who was married to Ava Gardner at the time, gave Lana the key to his house in Palm Springs. But Frank and Ava had another one of their famous fights. Before storming out of the house he shouted, "I'm leaving. And if you want to know where I am, I'm in Palm Springs fucking Lana Turner!"

Ava thought about what he said. She and Lana were pals, but Ava knew about Lana's previous affair with Frank and she made up her mind to catch them in the act. When Ava got to the house in Palm Springs, Frank was nowhere to be found, so she had a few drinks with Lana and her agent, Ben Cole. The girls were discussing Artie Shaw and Frank Sinatra when the latter walked into the house and heard the girls "really cutting me up."

He and Ava had another big fight, which was so loud and furious that a neighbor called the police. Lana said none of them mentioned that October night again because a vile rumor persisted after columnist Louella Parsons reported in a headline that "Frank Sinatra and Ava Gardner separate after he finds her with Lana Turner." The wording implies that he'd discovered the two women in bed together. Lana has denied the rumor, and there appears to be no truth to it. Regardless, Sinatra told Lana and Ava to leave the house, so they took off for a few days of fun in Mexico. (And two weeks later the columnist Earl Wilson printed a plea of love from Frank to Ava, and they reconciled.)

Lana returned to Hollywood and was seen on the nightclub circuit with Mexican bullfighter Luis Sallano and Lex Barker, who was separated from his second wife, actress Arlene Dahl.

On December 15, 1952, she appeared before Judge J. Guild in Carson City, Nevada. Wearing a clinging black dress and black fur coat, Lana charged Topping with mental cruelty and Judge Guild granted her a divorce. Reporters were waiting outside the courthouse for Lana, who said, "I'll never, never marry again!"

Lana went into another deep depression after the divorce, but she lacked the maturity to understand why she had lost Bob Topping, Tyrone Power, and Fernando Lamas. Perhaps she hadn't loved Bob enough, but she had been trying to save their marriage despite his drinking and carousing. Waiting for him to return, only to find out he was in love with someone else, bruised Lana's pride. She honestly thought Bob would come back. Instead, he was anxious to divorce her for another woman.

Fernando Lamas had no intention of marrying Lana. He'd used their romance to further his career and then beat her up when she deliberately flirted with another man in front of a crowd of Hollywood celebrities.

And of course, Lana would never get over the fact that Tyrone had married Linda Christian instead of her.

Once again Lana was fair game, but she was so wrapped up in her glamorous image, it never occurred to her that she might be to blame for her disastrous affairs and marriages. Mervyn LeRoy said, "I adored Lana, but she never grew up. That had a good deal to do with her perpetual youth and that wispy little-girl voice. What you saw on the screen was the real Lana Turner, and that's why she lasted.

Her fans were never disappointed to see her in person. But she was incapable of separating make-believe movies from real life. I don't think anyone dared tell her. L. B. Mayer, maybe, but she thought he was trying to keep her in line for the sake of MGM, not for her own good. Lana couldn't identify herself off the screen, and that's why she had so many ups and downs in her love life. I might add that men married Lana Turner the gorgeous movie star, and not Lana Turner the woman. I recall Bob Taylor telling me about his attraction to Lana years after *Johnny Eager* and admitting that he wasn't sophisticated enough to let his feelings cool down before proposing marriage. Most stars had to learn the same lesson, but not Lana. She believed moonlight and roses were eternal."

Lana was in debt after her divorce from Topping despite a hefty settlement. She owed back taxes and had to cut back drastically on her household staff. But she couldn't bear to budget her clothes allowance. She wouldn't be seen in the same dress more than once or twice. Lana's fetish for shoes was legendary as far back as her marriage to Artie Shaw. He had complained that she needed extra room for her clothes and shoes.

In view of Lana's financial problems, she was advised to live abroad for eighteen months to take advantage of the tax loophole that gave Americans immunity from paying taxes. MGM offered Lana *Mogambo*, with Clark Gable, but she didn't like the script so Ava Gardner got the part of Honey Bear. Lana regretted turning it down, even though her doctor thought it would be too risky in Africa if she got sick due to the Rh blood factor.

Another reason Lana did not want to spend six months in Africa was Lex Barker. After a few dates with the handsome, blond, six-foot-four actor, Lana was in love again. She chose to do *Flame and the Flesh* in Italy, where Barker was making two films.

The most popular hunk to portray Tarzan was Johnny Weissmuller, from 1932 until he became too old and flabby in 1948. Lex Barker then became the yodeling king of the jungle, whose most famous line was "Me Tarzan—you Jane." It didn't require much acting, just a magnificent physique and the ability to fly through the air hanging on to a vine in search of Jane and Cheeta.

Alexander Crichlow Barker was born in Rye, New York, in 1919, the only son of a socially prominent civil engineer. He attended Phillips Exeter Academy and Princeton University, and was a major in the infantry during the war. Rather than follow in his father's footsteps, Lex wanted to be an actor. After making four movies in Hollywood, he was chosen out of thousands of well-built men for Tarzan films at RKO.

Barker had two children, Lynne and Alexander Barker III, from his eight-year marriage to debutante Constance Thurlow. His second wife was the actress Arlene Dahl, whom he married in 1951. They were divorced the following year, and Arlene married none other than Fernando Lamas in 1954.

Lex grew tired of playing Tarzan and looked for better roles, which were not forthcoming. About the time Lana entered his life, he was offered films abroad because he could speak several languages fluently.

In April 1953, Lana and Lex left for Europe on separate planes. She hoped to make Paris her home base and to put ten-year-old Cheryl in a French school eventually. Lana rented two penthouse apartments and had the wall between them torn down. A close friend said, "Lana went abroad to save money and blew the profit right away. She *had* to live in luxury. I think Lana planned to marry Lex and stay in Europe, though she didn't say so. In fact, they tried to keep their big romance a secret, but everyone in Hollywood knew they were involved and would meet in Italy."

Lana's hair was dyed brown for *Flame and the Flesh*, and MGM began their publicity campaign with "That 'Bad and Beautiful Girl' is even more dangerous as a brunette." She plays a tramp who is rescued from the streets by a kindhearted singer (Carlos Thompson). They run away on the eve of his marriage to another girl (Pier Angeli). Lana loves him, but she realizes they could never be happy together. After sending him back home, she returns to the streets.

The *New York Herald Tribune* wrote, "Lana Turner has done the chic thing—she has made a film in Italy . . . [but] story-wise, the story is weak."

The *New York Times* thought the dialogue in *Flame and the Flesh* was corny but wrote, "Miss Turner is plenty fetching if not exactly noble. Although she is not precisely the femme fatale in delivering some of the lines that are her lot, her attributes are obviously superb."

Though Lex Barker's divorce from Arlene Dahl wasn't final, he wanted Lana to marry him in Europe. She felt three marriages were enough and was reluctant to give him an answer.

When she left Italy to film interior scenes for *Flame and the Flesh* in London, Lana and Lex were separated for several weeks. Ava Gardner, who had finished *Mogambo*, was also in England. The girls went on shopping sprees and attended parties together. One such gathering was an informal dinner given by director Tay Garnett and his wife. Sitting around having cocktails were Clark Gable, Sue and Alan Ladd, John Huston, and Robert Taylor. Ava whipped up some homemade chicken gravy for the group of celebrities who were hungry for some good old-fashioned American food.

But Lana was hungry for Barker. She returned to his villa in Italy and agreed to marry him. Lana had arrived with Cheryl and been greeted by Barker and his two children. From now on it was going to be one big happy family.

On September 8, 1953, Lana and Lex were married at the city hall in Turin, Italy. They spent a week's honeymoon on the isle of Capri and then returned to Lana's luxurious apartment in Paris. Plans had been made to put Cheryl in a Swiss school, but she rebelled. "I want to go home with Gran," Cheryl announced defiantly, and Mildred backed her up. Lana threatened to stop supporting her mother, but Mildred took Cheryl back to Los Angeles, and Barker's children returned to their mother.

Lana was angry and disappointed, but this was only the beginning of her problems as Mrs. Alexander Crichlow Barker.

Chapter 10

✳ HAPPY AT LAST? ✳

In October 1953, Lana and Clark Gable filmed *Betrayed* in Holland. This would be their last picture together, but, unfortunately, it was a disappointing war movie. Lana felt bad for Clark, because whenever they co-starred he was going through a major crisis. First it was Carole Lombard's death and then his sad homecoming from the war. Now it was a much older Gable, with his girth showing and his days numbered at MGM. Insiders knew the studio was not going to renew his contract. Lana did not approach the delicate subject with him, but she knew it was just a matter of time for her too. "The studios could no longer afford us," she commented. "We were all frightened."

Because there was so much publicity over Lana's dyed hair in *Flame and the Flesh*, she remained a brunette for *Betrayed*. The film might have had a chance if Lana and Clark had been allowed to light up the screen with some romantic fireworks, but their characters were too busy spying for the British during World War II. Critics panned the movie, concentrating on Gable for the most part. The *Hollywood Reporter* said, "Seeing Gable without sex is a good deal like seeing *Ben Hur* without horses." *Newsweek* reported that "Miss Turner plays her part of a spy with no conviction."

Lana changed her mind about staying in Europe for the required eighteen-month tax break. She gave up the Paris apartment, shipped her furniture back, and arrived home with Lex several days before Christmas. Another marriage ceremony was arranged "for family and friends," but the real reason for repeating their vows is that Barker's divorce from Arlene Dahl was not final when he'd married Lana in Italy. The "newlyweds" settled down in her house on Mapleton complete with a cook, maid, gardener, and governess. They owned a Cadillac convertible, a Jaguar, and a station wagon for family outings.

Mildred had taken a sales job after her spat with Lana in Paris, and she continued working even though they were living peacefully under the same roof.

Lana offered to use her influence to get Lex a contract at MGM, but he signed with Universal because, he said, "if anything happens to my marriage, I don't want to be thrown out like Lamas."

Hollywood considered Lana's fourth marriage a long shot, but columnists admitted that this one appeared to be more stable. Lana said in an interview, "I've never been married to an actor before." Moving a large bouquet of flowers that stood between her and Lex, she exclaimed, "He's brand new and I want to look at him." Lana hoped to have children because Barker's blood type was more compatible with hers. He told Hedda Hopper, "That's why she married me!"

*   *   *

Lana's first picture filmed in CinemaScope co-starred none other than Edmund Purdom, who was having an affair with Tyrone Power's wife, Linda Christian. *The Prodigal* was a $5 million production based on the biblical story about the son of a Hebrew farmer who falls under the spell of a high priestess (goddess of the flesh). With her hair bleached blond again, Lana was very, very fetching in the scanty costumes that barely got past the censors. One publicity shot that was used to promote *The Prodigal* showed Lana in nothing but G-strings and beads, and it had to be air-brushed before theater owners would display it.

Lana wasn't pleased with the picture, or with Edmund Purdom, whom she described as an egotist with garlic breath. The critics weren't impressed either, but there was much to be said for Lana's goddess of the flesh. Sidney Skolsky wrote in his column, "That long walk that Miss Turner takes through the Temple of Love in *The Prodigal* is the best reason for seeing the picture. Pure poetry in motion."

Bosley Crowther of the *New York Times* viewed the movie as a pompous, ostentatious, vulgar, and ridiculous charade. "Miss Turner conducts the rituals as though she were Little Egypt at the old Chicago's World Fair."

The day after Lana finished *The Prodigal*, she was rushed into *The Sea Chase*, with John Wayne. The star system was fading rapidly in the early 1950s. Lana was one of the few contract players left at MGM. While other stars were earning a percentage of the profits from their films, Lana was making $5,000 a week. There was, of course, the security of a regular paycheck, but she complained that MGM was making over $300,000 by loaning her out to Warner Brothers for *The Sea Chase*. Lana wasn't happy about filming on location in Hawaii without Lex, either. But she found John Wayne to be a true professional and a gentleman.

Lana played a German spy who falls in love with an anti-Nazi sea captain (Wayne). Casting these two stars together was a strange combination, but *The Sea Chase* was a success with their names on movie marquees.

As usual, there were rumors of a romance between Lana and John Wayne, but he was very much in love with his third wife, Pilar Palette, and Lana's heart belonged to Lex Barker, who was not behaving himself back on the mainland. Not only was he seeing other women, but he was taking advantage of ten-year-old Cheryl as well. His "lessons in sex" began with exposing himself and masturbating in front of her. Later Lex would come into Cheryl's bedroom and rape her. These violent sessions continued for three years, whether Lana was away or at home. Lex convinced Cheryl that she would go to juvenile hall if she told anyone.

After *The Sea Chase*, Lana and Lex spent a month in Acapulco at Ted Stauffer's secluded Villa Vera. Money was never a factor in Lana's marriages. She spent her own money freely, with or without a rich husband. She was always in debt to MGM because Lana lived beyond her means. During her marriage to Barker, it didn't faze him that she was a bigger name than he was. After his Tarzan films, Lex lost his star status. What kept him in the spotlight was being photographed with Lana at premieres and Hollywood parties. He had it made. While he repeatedly raped her daughter, Lana was having a wing built on the house for Barker's children, who came to live with them.

In the spring of 1955 Lana made a costume epic entitled *Diane*. She played the title role of Diane de Poitiers, the mistress of King Henri II of France (Roger Moore). This would be her last picture filmed at the MGM studios, though Lana didn't know it at the time. *Diane* was a colorful movie and well received. As usual, Lana was acclaimed for her beauty and magnificent costumes.

Under her contract with MGM, she owed them one more picture, and she was loaned out to 20th Century-Fox for *The Rains of Ranchipur*, a remake of *The Rains Came*. Shortly before filming began in August, she slipped in the shower, hit her head, and suffered a concussion. Two weeks later she was still plagued with dizziness and headaches, but producer Frank Ross was willing to wait for Lana and nurse her through the film.

The theme of *The Rains of Ranchipur* is a romance between the selfish wife of a titled Englishman and a dedicated Indian doctor, played by Richard Burton. A camera crew went to India to shoot background settings, but the cast filmed in Hollywood.

Lana said there was no chemistry between her and Burton, whom she described as a supreme egoist. Though he was famous for romancing his leading ladies, Lana did not complain about any advances on his part. His style was much like Clark Gable's: If he couldn't seduce his leading lady, there were plenty of cute extras on the set. (Six years later Burton would become involved with Elizabeth Taylor during *Cleopatra*.)

The Rains of Ranchipur received mixed reviews. The New York *Daily News* gave it a four-star rating. The *New York Times* hailed Burton's performance and described Lana as never looking lovelier, while *Redbook* chose *Rains* as the "picture of the month" (December 1955).

✳   ✳   ✳

MGM did not renew Lana's contract in February 1956. She claimed that she left of her own volition because the studio put her in rotten pictures. "I'm tired of costume epics," she said. But it didn't matter who dropped whom, because it was a sad day when Lana packed up her belongings and left Metro-Goldwyn-Mayer for the last time. It had been her second home for eighteen years. She had been primed, protected, pampered, and literally treated like a queen. Like so many stars, Lana was bitter at first, complaining that being under contract to Metro was like being in jail. In time, however, she realized how much she had taken for granted: limousines, hairdressers, fashion designers, first-class accommodations on planes, trains, and at hotels, publicists who shielded her from the press, the Christmas parties with Gardner, Taylor, Gable, Tracy, and so many others whom she loved dearly. Except for Elizabeth Taylor, Esther Williams, Robert Taylor, and a select few remaining under contract, the MGM studios were lifeless.

That year, 1956, was not a good one for Lana. She was forced to pay back her sizable loans to Metro, leaving her short of money. She became pregnant again but the child, a girl, was stillborn in her seventh month. While she recuperated in the hospital, depressed and weak, Lex was sneaking into Cheryl's bedroom.

It took Lana a while to find a suitable film. She finally settled for *The Lady Takes a Flyer*, with Jeff Chandler at Universal. In this picture Lana is a flying instructor who falls in love and marries a pilot (Chandler). When she has a baby and is forced to stay home, he continues flying in more ways than one. She forces him to stay home and play "Mommy" while she returns to the sky. The ending is a comical and happy one.

The Lady Takes a Flyer was a pleasant and amusing film. Lana and Jeff Chandler were right for each other on the screen, but Barker accused her of seeing Chandler after hours. Perhaps he suspected her of doing the same thing as he was—seeing others on the sly. Lana had heard rumors about other women, but she was used to Hollywood gossip. Despite their bickering, Lana became pregnant again but had another miscarriage.

MGM press agent George Nichols said, "I think they were both playing around at this point. Barker was on location most of the time and would be gone for weeks. I know for a fact that Lana was doing the nightclub scene. She wasn't the type to sit home alone. Nor did she like being without a man for long."

In early 1957, Cheryl decided not to take any more punishment from Lex. He had become so violent, she feared for her health and sanity. Cheryl confided in a friend, who urged her to tell someone. That someone was Mildred, who in turn confronted Lana about the outrage. They had Cheryl examined, and the doctor confirmed that the thirteen-year-old had been injured internally.

Lana found Lex relaxing in bed. He didn't see her come into the room with a gun. Was she going to kill him? No, but she wanted to. Instead, Lana got hold of herself, told him she knew about his attacks on Cheryl, and gave Lex twenty minutes to get out of the house. He obliged, but a few days later he begged Lana to change her mind "because the kid's lying to you." She turned her back on him and filed for divorce.

Lex told the press he blamed Cheryl for the breakup of his marriage. "She told lies about me," he said. "She's a bad girl and will end up in real trouble one day."

Barker settled in Europe and became an international star, with homes in Spain, Switzerland, and Italy. On May 11, 1973, he collapsed of a massive heart attack on Lexington Avenue near 61st Street in New York City at the age of fifty-three. When Lana heard the news she said, "What took him so long?"

A month after her separation from Barker, Lana went to Palm Springs for the weekend with a young actor in his early twenties. Newsmen identified him as Michael Dante, whom Lana was trying to get into films.

Cheryl joined her mother, and they quarreled for two days. Lana was in a black mood over being dropped by MGM and going through another divorce. After a few drinks she accused Cheryl of "tantalizing" Lex and slapped her across the face. Driving back to Los Angeles, Lana continued to nag Cheryl, who got out of the car before they reached home. She roamed around Skid Row and allowed herself to be picked up by a man who turned her in as a runaway. Lana was furious. "What am I going to do with you?" she cried. Cheryl solved that problem by moving in with Mildred.

Lana leased her house on Mapleton and put it up for sale. There were too many bad memories of her marriages to Topping and Barker, and the upkeep was too expensive. Some of the furniture went into storage and Lana moved into a penthouse apartment off Wilshire Boulevard.

On April 15, 1957, Louella Parsons wrote in her column that the luscious Lana Turner had signed with producer Jerry Wald to play the mother of an eighteen-year-old in *Peyton Place*, based on the best-selling novel by Grace

Metalious. The part of Constance MacKenzie was one of the best Lana had played in a long time. Pretending to be a widow, Constance brings up her daughter, Allison, in a small New England town where everyone knows everyone else's business. That she was never married is a secret until Constance, in the heat of an argument, reveals the truth to Allison, who leaves home. *Peyton Place* is filled with rape, vicious gossip, sex, love, and murder. Today the book and the film would be run of the mill, but in 1957 it shocked the world that such scandal could take place in small-town America.

Ironically, Lana's role as the mother who is so protective of her daughter that it leads to estrangement mirrored her current relationship with Cheryl.

Peyton Place was released in December 1957 and nominated for nine Oscars, among them a best actress for Lana Turner. The picture was a hit at the box office and with the critics. It revived Lana's career and her stature in Hollywood.

Chapter 11

✳ STOMPANATO ✳

IN THE SPRING OF 1957 LANA BEGAN RE-
ceiving repeated phone calls from a man who called himself
John Steele. She ignored them. Soon he was sending flowers nearly every day with the same card, signed John Steele
with his telephone number. Lana became curious about
the mystery man when the calls and flowers continued.
Finally she phoned Steele, who said he was an admirer and
asked, "How about dinner?" She refused, but he didn't
give up. Lana liked his voice and the expensive flowers he
sent regularly, as well as the thoughtful gifts such as her
favorite record albums that she played in her dressing room.
Apparently John Steele had access to people close to Lana,
but more important, he had taken the time to find out
everything about her. She called him again to say her dressing room was overflowing with flowers and not to bother
sending more, but Steele asked again if she would have
lunch or cocktails with him, and Lana gave in. All right,
he could drop by her place later in the evening for a drink,
but she insisted he call first because she was working late
at the studio. Instead she found Steele waiting in his black
Lincoln Continental when she left work. They had a drink
and he left.

More flowers and more phone calls from the handsome but mysterious John Steele. Lana didn't want to be seen with a stranger in public, so she invited him for lunch at her apartment. He offered to bring the food, and it turned out to be a dish from one of Lana's favorite restaurants. Before he arrived she received a diamond bracelet from Steele, who refused to take it back "because it's engraved." They began seeing each other off and on, and each time he came to see her, Steele gave Lana another piece of expensive jewelry. And flowers arrived every day on the movie set. After several weeks of courting, they became intimate. Lana was seeing other men in the summer of 1957, but by September John Steele wanted her all to himself, and Lana didn't resist. She was in love.

Though they were not seen together in public, there are no secrets in Hollywood. A friend told Lana, "The man you're dating is Johnny Stompanato. He has connections with gangster Mickey Cohen."

She approached her lover who called himself John Steele. "Are you really Johnny Stompanato?" she asked.

"So what?" he said with a laugh.

"Why did you lie to me?"

"Because I knew you wouldn't see me if I gave my real name."

"That's true, and now I have my doubts," she said.

"It's too late," he said, smirking. "You're mine now."

When Lana was in love with a man she made allowances, and clearly she was deeply involved with Johnny Stompanato. He was right: It *was* too late.

Cheryl liked him too. Aware that she liked horses, he gave her carte blanche to his stable. He also offered her a summer job in his gift shop, supposedly Johnny's only means of support. He was very kind to Cheryl and he won her over in no time. Lana had confided in Johnny about

Lex Barker's abuse, so he was careful not to get overly affectionate. Cheryl admitted in her book, *Detour*, that she preferred girls anyway. Before Barker's attacks she had already fallen in love with a girlfriend, but at such a young age Cheryl knew nothing about lesbianism.

Johnny Stompanato, the son of a barber, was born on October 19, 1925, in Woodstock, Illinois, the youngest of four. His mother died shortly after he was born. John attended Kemper Military Academy, graduated at the age of seventeen, and joined the Marines in 1943. He saw action in Okinawa and wound up in Tientsin, a port in northeastern China. There he met Sarah Utich, a Turkish woman six years older. He married her in a Muslim ceremony and took her home to Woodstock, where she gave birth to a son, John III. A year later Stompanato got restless and headed for California. Sarah sued him for divorce on the grounds of desertion.

Johnny, who was five-foot-eleven and weighed 180 pounds, got a job as a bouncer in one of Mickey Cohen's Hollywood nightclubs. He became friendly with his boss and was soon working as a bodyguard for $300 a week. Stompanato was arrested six times on various charges, but never convicted.

His next marriage, in 1949, to actress Helen Gilbert, lasted three months. She was eight years older than Johnny. In 1953 he married actress Helen Stanley, also considerably older, and they were divorced two years later. By now Johnny had a reputation as a gigolo in Hollywood. He dressed like a million dollars, hung out in nightclubs, and had no problem attracting wealthy women. Stompanato was a good-looking Italian with piercing brown eyes, black wavy hair, and a strong physique. He was smooth, egotistical, and a cocksure lover.

Johnny got the money to finance his "front," the Myrtlewood Gift Shop, from a widow who defended his honor. She said the money was a loan, and he never made any advances toward her.

By the fall of 1957 Lana knew her reputation was at stake if she flaunted her affair with Johnny, so they were rarely photographed together.

According to a friend, Lana gave Johnny an ID bracelet inscribed "My love and my life. Lanita." She lavished other gifts on him. Money too. Once he had won her over, Lana was the one who paid. She had formed her own production company, Lanturn, and Johnny hoped to co-produce and share in the profits. Whether Lana ever gave him the impression she would go along with this business arrangement isn't known. As much as she loved Stompanato, Lana feared he could be dangerous if provoked. When she told him about filming *Another Time, Another Place* in England at the end of the year, Johnny wanted to accompany her. She said his presence might interfere with her concentration and told (or asked) him to stay home.

In November Lana flew to London. She wrote passionate letters to Johnny and he called regularly, begging to join her. Finally Lana gave in and arranged for an airline ticket. Johnny stayed at her rented house in Hampstead Heath. While she worked, he had use of her limousine for sightseeing and shopping. The studio, however, was off-limits. Except for a few co-workers, Lana did not want anyone to know about Stompanato.

Another Time, Another Place is about a woman's affair

with a married man. Lana's lover in this tearjerker is Sean Connery, a British actor then relatively unknown in America. After his character's death in a plane crash, Lana has a nervous breakdown. During her recovery she visits his hometown in England where, by accident, she becomes friendly with her late lover's wife and child. Eventually Lana admits an affair with her husband but assures the widow he loved his family most of all.

As usual, there was gossip about Lana and Sean Connery. They were rather close off the set, and it was taken for granted that there was a romance brewing. Stompanato somehow heard about Lana's frequent cocktail dates with Connery and, in a jealous rage, appeared on the movie set with a gun in his hand. He confronted Connery, who landed a right to Johnny's nose, knocking him helplessly to the floor. When he managed to get to his feet he was "escorted" out of the studio.

Johnny might have sought revenge on Connery. Instead, he fought with Lana and nearly choked her to death. During the Christmas holidays, he pressed the issue of becoming her business partner. When she hedged, Stompanato put a pillow over her face. If a maid hadn't heard screams he might have smothered her.

The choking episode affected Lana's vocal chords. She suffered a bruised larynx and couldn't talk for a while. Production was held up for a few days until she recovered from laryngitis. Only her associate producer and long-time friend Del Armstrong knew the truth. When Johnny threatened Lana again it was Armstrong who urged her to call Scotland Yard and have Stompanato deported. Two policemen drove Johnny to the airport and remained there until he was aboard and the plane had taken off. He phoned Lana repeatedly from home, and it didn't take her very long before she called him back, followed by love letters and many more phone calls urging Stompanato to spend a few weeks with her in Acapulco when she finished *Another Time, Another Place.*

Lonely and unhappy, Lana had Cheryl flown to London for the Christmas holidays. They were excited about an invitation from Buckingham Palace for a presentation to Queen Elizabeth and Prince Philip, but it was canceled. Apparently the Stompanato incident did not sit well with Palace officials.

In mid-January 1958, Cheryl flew back to Los Angeles. On her way to Acapulco, Lana had a stopover in Copenhagen, where Johnny was waiting. Though he did not sit with her during a press conference at the airport, his reason for being there was obvious to reporters.

In her memoirs, Lana insisted she was shocked to find Stompanato waiting for her in Denmark. According to reliable sources, however, she'd not only pleaded with him to meet her but also picked up the tab for their vacation in Mexico. Lana told a friend she had second thoughts about seeing Johnny again and sent him a letter telling him to forget about Mexico, but it arrived after his departure for Copenhagen.

Lana had reserved a suite at Teddy Stauffer's Villa Vera before she knew Johnny was coming along. For propriety's sake she insisted he stay in another room, but the only one available was no bigger than a closet and it had no bathroom. He was furious, but Lana insisted he keep it, even though they stayed in her suite for the most part. By now Stompanato was growing tired of hiding in the shadows with Lana. He wanted to marry her, pay off his debts, and share the limelight. He wanted control of her body, soul, and bank account.

During Lana's two months in Acapulco, observers said she was always with Johnny. He never took his eyes off her, out of either love or jealousy. At times she seemed tense, almost afraid of Johnny, but the consensus was that Lana loved him very much. Where he went, she followed, taking his hand or sitting on his lap.

Lana had another cause to be happy. She'd found out about her Oscar nomination for best actress in *Peyton Place* and concentrated on a suntan for her appearance at the Academy Awards ceremony in April.

This was a bittersweet stage in Lana's life. She knew her affair with Stompanato was wrong. He was using and abusing her. Yet she was hooked and incapable of giving him up. She began drinking heavily in Mexico to get through this bewildering situation. One night she was tired and wanted to be alone. Johnny smashed down the door. On another occasion he put a gun to her head because she refused to have sex with him.

Half drunk most of the time, Lana did not resist being seen with Johnny in public. Word got back to Hollywood, and Louella Parsons wrote in her column, "I hope it isn't true that Lana Turner, who is now in Acapulco, is going to marry Johnny Stompanato."

A week before the Academy Awards, Lana and Johnny flew back to Los Angeles. Mildred and Cheryl were at the airport to meet them. The press was there too, but this time Stompanato took Lana's arm and smiled broadly. Photographers asked Cheryl to pose with them, and she obliged by putting her arm around Johnny's waist. The next day newspapers headlined Lana's affair with mobster Johnny Stompanato, a former associate of Mickey Cohen. She denied a romantic involvement.

Lana made it perfectly clear to Johnny that he would not accompany her to the Oscar ceremony. At first he turned on the charm, buying thoughtful trinkets for Lana (charged to her account) and reverting to the romantic fellow who'd won her over in the beginning. When she didn't give in, he begged and then threatened her. "It's going to be a family evening," Lana told him. "Mother, Cheryl, and me."

"No parties afterward," he warned.

Lana had given up her penthouse apartment on Wilshire Boulevard and was staying in a bungalow at the Bel-Air Hotel until she could find a house in Beverly Hills. The night of the Academy Awards, March 24, 1958, Lana's hairdresser and seamstress fussed over her while John watched with a scowl on his face. She was a vision, in a clinging strapless white-lace sheath that flared out in three tiers below the knees, diamond earrings, a diamond bracelet, diamond necklace, and a few diamonds on her fingers. Many of these fabulous jewels had been gifts from Bob Topping.

At the Pantages Theater, Lana presented the award for best supporting actor to Red Buttons for *Sayonara*. She was trembling as the names for best actress were announced and scenes with her in *Peyton Place* were shown. But it was Joanne Woodward who won for her performance in *Three Faces of Eve.*

Lana accepted defeat graciously. After the award ceremony she took Cheryl to the ball at the Beverly Hilton Hotel. Like old times, Lana held court at her table and danced with Clark Gable and Sean Connery, to name a few. For Lana this was an evening of reminiscing with old friends whom she hadn't seen in a long time, and she took advantage of every minute of the Hollywood splendor that was slowly fading for the Golden Era movie greats.

Cheryl came back to the Bel-Air Hotel to spend the night with Lana. Too excited to sleep, they sat up talking about the famous guests who'd fawned over Lana: Cary Grant, John Wayne, Gregory Peck, Jimmy Stewart, and Sean Connery. Lana told Cheryl about the house she was renting beginning April 1. "It's on Bedford Drive," she explained, "and it has a tennis court in back. You'll have a nice big room with a fireplace, and I think it's time you had your own telephone."

Cheryl pretended to be pleased, but she'd have to think about living with a mother who was so very strict. Lana raised objections to Cheryl's smoking and wearing makeup, but she put up with it because they saw very little of each other. Living under the same roof might involve severe restrictions, but since Cheryl assumed Stompanato was going to be her stepfather, she knew he'd take her side and everything would work out just fine.

Lana retired to her bedroom and found Johnny waiting there. He had been listening to her and Cheryl talking about the party and was livid that he had been banned from this prestigious event. Lana told him to leave. He slapped her so hard she hit the floor. He picked her up and hit her in the face. As she was still wearing her diamond earrings, the stones cut into her cheeks. He punched her body, knocked her down again, picked her up, and socked her once more. He threw her on the bed and she pleaded with him to stop. "If you promise never to go anywhere without me again!" he snarled, sitting on her stomach. She nodded and he let her go. In the bathroom, Lana rinsed her mouth, which was full of blood. Her cheeks were bruised and her jaw was turning purple. Weak and sick to her stomach, she got into bed and pretended to be asleep. She said he waited before kissing her on the cheek and leaving the bungalow.

Cheryl had heard loud voices but had no idea that her mother had been brutally beaten. A few days later she overheard vicious words exchanged between Johnny and

Lana. Cheryl was shocked by his threats and filthy lan-
guage. He had always been soft-spoken, warm and kind to
her. What was going on? This time Cheryl asked her
mother, "Is something wrong between you and Johnny?"
Lana broke down and told her the truth. She couldn't tell
the police because Johnny had threatened to have Cheryl
and Mildred killed. He'd threatened to disfigure her face
with a razor. If he were arrested, Johnny would have one
of his gangster friends carry out these threats.

Cheryl was only fourteen and she tried to grasp what
was happening. The next day, April 2, Johnny helped to
move her belongings from Mildred's apartment into the
newly rented house on Bedford Drive. Lana was civil to
him, and for the next few days they were busy moving,
shopping, and getting settled.

It came out later that Lana had confided in Mildred,
who'd called their friend Chief Anderson at the police department. "I can't do anything unless Lana makes a formal
complaint," he told Mildred. "Please ask her to call me."
But Lana never did.

Chapter 12

✳ MURDER AT
730 NORTH BEDFORD DRIVE? ✳

$\mathcal{G}$OOD FRIDAY, APRIL 4, 1958. A RAINY, gloomy day in Beverly Hills. Cheryl had lunch with her father and Lana went shopping with Johnny for kitchen necessities. Her invited cocktail guests, Del Armstrong and a friend, Bill Brooks, were already at the Bedford house when she arrived home. While Johnny took the packages into the kitchen, Brooks told Lana, "I know Stompanato. How did you get mixed up with a guy like that?"

"How do you know John?" she asked.

"We went to military school together."

"How old are you, Bill?"

"Thirty-five."

"But John's much older," Lana commented. "How could you have been in school together?"

"I was two years ahead of him," Brooks said. "He's around thirty-three."

"Strange," she exclaimed. "John told me he was forty-three."

Stompanato had left the house in the meantime, apparently uncomfortable in the presence of Bill Brooks. When he returned, Lana confronted him about his age. "Another lie?" she asked sarcastically.

"So what?" he said with a smirk. "I thought we were going to a movie."

"I'm not in the mood," she said.

"I suppose you'd rather stay home and get drunk again."

"Just leave me alone," she snapped.

He followed her upstairs and into Cheryl's bedroom. "Johnny's leaving," Lana announced.

"You're not getting rid of me," he snarled.

"How many times have I told you not to argue in front of the baby!"

"I think she's old enough to know the truth about her mother," he said.

Lana told Cheryl, "I'm going downstairs to get a drink honey. I'll be right back. Johnny has to leave."

He followed her downstairs. They argued about her drinking too much and then Lana went upstairs to her bedroom with a drink and locked the door.

"Open up, bitch!" he shouted. "Or I'll break the fuckin' door down!"

Lana knew he was strong enough to do it, so she let him in. Cheryl heard Johnny shouting, "You'll never get rid of me! I'll cut you up first."

Cheryl knocked on the door and took Lana by the hand into another room. "Get rid of him, Mother. Why don't you just stand up to him?"

"Because I'm deathly afraid of John," Lana said breathlessly. "But it has to be done, I guess."

"I'm here," Cheryl said, trying to comfort her mother.

Lana went back to her bedroom and told Stompanato there was nothing to talk about. "This is a new house—a new start for me. I don't want you here. Please go."

He spun Lana around and grabbed her by the shoulders. "You can't order me around!" he ranted. "I give the orders. If I tell you to jump, you'll jump. If I tell you to hop, you'll hop!"

Cheryl was standing in the hall near her mother's room. She heard Johnny threaten, "You'll never get away from me. I'll find you. I'll cut up your face. You'll never work again. I'll get your mother and daughter too. I told you once I can find the right people to take care of them."

Cheryl ran down the stairs, not knowing why. Call the police? Call her father? No, they might not get here in time. She went into the kitchen and saw a butcher knife on the counter. That's it. I'll scare him, she thought. I'll frighten him away.

Cheryl took the knife upstairs and put it on the floor near her mother's bedroom. Lana was crying hysterically now, pleading with Johnny to leave. "It's the end for you," he yelled.

"Get out!" she shrieked.

"You're dead, bitch," he shouted.

Cheryl picked up the knife and pounded on the door. "Mother, please! Let me talk to you both. Please!"

Lana opened the door. Her hand was on the knob as Johnny raised his arm to hit her. Cheryl took a step into the room with the knife in her hand. She explained later, "Johnny ran on the blade. It went in. He looked straight at me and said, 'My God, Cheryl, what have you done?' "

Stompanato took three tiny steps backward, his eyes frozen on Cheryl, and then he fell backward onto the floor. She dropped the bloody knife and ran to her own bedroom. Lana heard Johnny choking and gurgling but saw no wound until she pulled up his sweater. In shock, she picked up the knife and put it in the bathroom sink, then she got a towel to cover Stompanato's wound. "Speak to me, John!" No answer. Lana tried breathing into his mouth, but he lay motionless. Frantically, she phoned Mildred. "Get a doctor over here right away! Don't ask any questions. Hurry!"

Cheryl called her father. "Daddy, it's John. Something awful has happened. Come quick!"

Stephan Crane was the first to arrive at 730 North Bedford Drive. Cheryl sobbed over and over again, "I did it. I didn't mean to do it. I'm sorry. I didn't mean to do it. I'm sorry."

Mildred tried to help Lana revive John by breathing into his mouth. Dr. McDonald arrived and gave Stompanato a shot of adrenaline into the heart, then called an ambulance. Cheryl was trembling and mumbling, "I'm so sorry. I didn't mean to do it. . . ." When Dr. McDonald came into her room, she asked, "Will John be all right?"

"He's gone, Cheryl. I'm going to give you a sedative, but everything will be just fine. Your dad will stay here with you for a while."

The doctor took Lana aside and whispered, "You'd better call a lawyer. I suggest Jerry Geisler. He's the best."

Geisler had successfully defended Errol Flynn and Charlie Chaplin on statutory rape charges. Lana had to track him down at a dinner party, but he rushed to her house and got there shortly before the police.

Chief Anderson spoke to Lana, who tried to take the blame for Stompanato's death. He said, "We already know Cheryl did it."

Squad cars, ambulances, and members of the press surrounded the house. Police photographers took pictures of Stompanato's lifeless body while Cheryl and Lana prepared to go to the Beverly Hills police station. Leaving the house was hectic, and they had to brave popping flash bulbs and questions by eager reporters. More humiliating was posing for cameramen at Chief Anderson's office.

Cheryl, half drugged, explained how frightened she

was for her mother, how she'd tried to protect Lana when John raised his arm to hit her.

In Lana's version, there is a discrepancy, though she didn't realize it at the time. "John was holding a jacket and shirt on hangers behind him when Cheryl came in," she said. In other words, he was leaving and his arm was not raised to strike Lana.

Chief Anderson said Cheryl would have to spend the night in jail. Stephen and Lana raised a fuss, but Geisler said they could take her home in the morning. Lana said she never forgot seeing Cheryl behind bars before she was forced to leave. Almost as devastating was her arriving home with Geisler just in time to see Stompanato's body being carried out of the house.

"Oh, God!" Lana cried out.

"Get down!" Geisler told her. "And stay down." He got out of his car and told reporters that Lana was spending the night elsewhere.

At the police station, mob boss Mickey Cohen made a ruckus about the "murder" of his friend. He told reporters there was something fishy about Cheryl's story. Cohen was also suspicious about Lana's offer to take the rap for her daughter. "Johnny was too smart," Cohen said. "They say he didn't defend himself. It don't make sense."

Perhaps one of Cheryl's most troubling statements was her telling Lana, "You don't have to take that, Mother."

The pressure was on Chief Anderson. He knew it was expected of him to give Lana Turner's daughter a break. She should get preferential treatment. That might have been possible if there were not conflicting stories that had already leaked to the press overnight. In the morning Cheryl Crane was booked on suspicion of murder. If convicted as a juvenile, she would face life imprisonment. Bail was denied and Cheryl went to the juvenile hall. Lana and

Stephen Crane made headlines when they paid her a visit on Easter Sunday, arriving and leaving in separate cars. It was also reported that Frank Sinatra was one of the first to call on Lana to see if there was anything he could do.

The curious drove past 730 North Bedford Drive every hour of the day. But that was the least of Lana's worries. Carmine Stompanato had a long meeting with Chief Anderson before his brother's funeral. Mickey Cohen swore vengeance and urged Carmine to "demand a complete investigation" into John's death. Lana was given police protection around the clock.

Meanwhile Geisler's defense was "justifiable homicide." He denied that an hour had lapsed after John was stabbed before the police and doctor were called to the house.

Mildred stayed with Lana, who was in shock and hysterical, despite the sedatives administered by Dr. McDonald. Friends said the beautiful Lana had aged overnight, and was looking haggard and drawn. But Geisler made sure she was prepared for the predetention hearing.

Just hours after Stompanato's death was announced, someone broke into his apartment. No valuables were taken, so it was unclear what the burglar wanted. Five days later, however, this mystery was partially solved when Lana's love letters to Johnny were published in the *Los Angeles Herald Examiner*. Mickey Cohen admitted giving them to the newspaper but denied taking them from Stompanato's apartment. "They were given to me," Cohen said, "and I gave them to the *Examiner* because I wanted to prove that Johnny's attentions to Lana were not exactly unwelcome."

The letters were damaging to Cheryl's defense and to Lana's reputation. She wrote to Johnny about her deep love for him, how she ached to be with him, referring to him as "My Beloved Love" and "My Dearest Darling Love." There were letters from Cheryl to Johnny also, ending with "Love ya and miss ya." Stretching the imagination, there was a hint that Cheryl could have been intimate with Stompanato, and perhaps her motive for the stabbing was jealousy.

Lana's letters were those of a gushy young girl in love with love, yearning for "her man's" phone calls and to be "cuddled" by him.

Publication of the letters coincided with Stompanato's funeral on April 9 in Woodstock, New York. Dressed in a tuxedo, he was buried with full military honors. Mickey Cohen, who was in the thirteen-limousine cortege, paid for everything "because Johnny was used to nothing but the best."

Lana's twelve letters to Stompanato were printed in newspapers from coast to coast for two days.

Another Time, Another Place was released three months earlier than scheduled, to take advantage of Lana's off-screen notoriety. The picture did not do well at the box office, however. If Lana's character had been more amorous and sexy, the public might have gone to see it. She was, in fact, dull in the film, as opposed to the daily newspaper headlines about her notorious affair with the gangster who was killed in her bedroom.

Hollywood insiders were divided in their feelings toward Lana. They were aware of her many affairs but thought she had lowered herself by going with Stompanato. Obviously, they concluded, he was a well-endowed lover. Otherwise Lana would have turned him away at the outset.

*　❋　❋

It was a sweltering 86° on Friday, April 11, when hundreds of hopeful spectators lined up outside the Hall of Records courtroom for the inquest. Cheryl did not have to testify, thanks to Jerry Geisler, who said she was a juvenile and he did not want her to go through the trauma again. So Lana was the star witness.

Mickey Cohen took the stand first.

"Were you able to identify your former bodyguard?" the deputy coroner asked.

"I refuse to identify the body on the grounds I may be accused of murder," Cohen responded, chewing on a wad of gum.

The coroner repeated the question. Mickey repeated his answer and was then dismissed.

Dr. McDonald was the next witness in the hot and muggy courtroom. He identified Stompanato's body and said the eight-inch blade had punctured the abdomen, kidney, and aorta. McDonald said Johnny had died within a few minutes. No one could have saved his life.

Lana, wearing a tailored gray suit, was on the stand for an hour. She recounted the argument with Stompanato and how she walked toward the bedroom door. He was behind her. "I opened the door and my daughter walked in. I thought it was so fast. I thought she hit him in the stomach. They came together and then they parted. I never saw the blade. Mr. Stompanato grabbed his abdomen, started to move forward, took a half turn, and then dropped on his back." Lana went on to describe how she'd tried to revive him by breathing into his mouth. Dr. McDonald said he had worked on Stompanato for several minutes and said, "I can't get a heartbeat."

It took the jury only twenty-five minutes to come up with a verdict of justifiable homicide. Cheryl, however, would have to face a juvenile court hearing on April 21.

One of the most shocking revelations at the inquest was the coroner's report that Stompanato had had a serious liver ailment that would have killed him in a matter of a few years.

Lana's ordeal was not over. Newspapers labeled her an unfit mother. The *Los Angeles Times* wrote, "In the Turner case Cheryl isn't the juvenile delinquent; Lana is."

Hedda Hopper got even with Lana by ignoring her after the verdict: "My heart bleeds for Cheryl."

In his syndicated column Walter Winchell wrote, "She is made of rays of the sun, woven of blue eyes. Honey-colored hair and flowing curves. She is Lana Turner, goddess of the screen. . . . Give your heart to the girl with the broken heart."

Actress Gloria Swanson shot back at Winchell: "I think it's disgusting that you are trying to whitewash Lana. She is not even an actress. . . . She is only a trollop."

The press was unanimous about one aspect: Lana's testimony was the most dramatic scene of her life.

Stephan Crane, who stood by his daughter and ex-wife, collapsed after the inquest. He was reportedly on the verge of a nervous breakdown.

Cheryl remained at the juvenile hall, not knowing what the future held for her, reform school or maybe a foster home. District Attorney McKesson decided not to prosecute her, but he made a statement that Cheryl had never had a real home, "either with her mother or her father."

Crane backed Lana, saying he would not seek custody of Cheryl, but he changed his mind.

On April 24, Judge Lynch asked Cheryl which parent she preferred living with if it were up to her. Lana and Crane were shocked when their daughter replied, "I want to live with my grandmother."

The judge determined that Cheryl would be a ward of the court until she was eighteen. For the next sixty days she would live with Mildred. Lana and Crane were granted visiting rights only once a week.

Chapter 13

✴ STARTING OVER ✴

$\mathcal{L}$ANA HAD WON THE BATTLE BUT LOST THE war. She was heavily in debt to MGM and to Jerry Geisler. There were two suits against her by the Stompanatos, and her production company had lost money from *Another Time, Another Place*.

She had moved out of the Bedford Drive house and rented another one on Canon Drive that she turned over to her mother and daughter. Lana moved into Mildred's apartment, where she remained secluded, with the shades down. She ventured out only with Jerry Geisler to testify in her own defense against the Stompanatos, who claimed that Johnny was stabbed when he was lying down. They based this on the fact that Cheryl was in the doorway with a knife and Johnny's body lay near the bed. If he had been wounded standing up, why wasn't there any blood below his waist? And why didn't Lana step in and prevent Cheryl from stabbing Johnny? The case was eventually settled two years later for $20,000.

In need of money, Lana wasn't sure how to proceed with her career. Would anyone in Hollywood take a chance on her after the Stompanato scandal? Producer Ross Hunter did, but he had a difficult time convincing Lana to do *Imitation of Life*, the story of an actress who gives up her daughter and the man she loves for her career. "I can't do it," Lana said. "The theme is too close to home."

Hunter said kindly, "You'll have to face life sometime, dear. It's a great role and I think people will admire you more for doing it."

Lana went back to work for $2,500 a week and a percentage of the profits. If the picture failed, her career would most likely be finished. But Lana liked and trusted Hunter, and she forged ahead with the heavy task of reliving her life on the screen. Co-starring in the film were John Gavin as Lana's lover, Sandra Dee as her sixteen-year-old daughter, Juanita Moore as Lana's black maid and friend, and Susan Kohner as Juanita's eighteen-year-old daughter.

Based on Fannie Hurst's novel, *Imitation of Life* is a real tearjerker. Sandra Dee falls in love with Lana's lover, and Kohner resents her black heritage. When Moore dies at the end, Kohner runs after the hearse, pleading forgiveness. At the conclusion, Lana and Gavin are reunited, with her daughter's blessing.

The movie was a box-office smash. *Imitation of Life* made more money than any other film at Universal ever had, and it put Lana back on her feet financially. Kohner and Moore were nominated for Oscars.

While Lana was filming during the summer of 1958, she accepted an invitation to a party—one of the very few she attended after Johnny's death. She was immediately attracted to a man who resembled Tyrone Power, but she did not make her usual effort to eye him. Eventually she was introduced to Fred May, a real-estate tycoon. Their brief conversation was casual until May mentioned his ranch, where he raised thoroughbreds for racing. Lana perked up, saying she loved horses and would like to see the ranch sometime. He asked for her telephone number but did not make a note of it. Perhaps that was just as well, Lana concluded. She was reluctant to get involved with another man so soon, but when May called her several days later, she accepted an invitation to see his ranch.

They had a long talk over dinner at his apartment. Fred admitted his attraction to her at the party, but he'd been shy about calling for a date because he was going through a messy divorce. Though Lana had moved into a house on Roxbury Drive, she was soon living with May at his ranch.

She went on a publicity tour for *Imitation of Life* reluctantly, fearing the public would not accept her. Lana was also fearful of Mickey Cohen's mob friends, but the tour was a safe and successful one. She also had an innocent fling in Chicago—proof that Lana Turner was indeed her old self again.

Returning to California, she accepted another movie offer from Ross Hunter, *Portrait in Black*. Lana fares very well as an adulterous wife who murders her wealthy husband with the help of her lover (Anthony Quinn). Mysterious letters from someone claiming to know who the killer is plague the couple, bringing them closer together. But it is Lana who wrote the letters to cement her relationship with Quinn, who in his fury goes after her and falls to his death from a window ledge. Lana's stepdaughter (Sandra Dee) witnesses everything, and it is Lana who has to face the murder of her husband alone.

Portrait in Black was another financial bonanza for Ross Hunter and Lana, despite what the critics had to say.

Like old times, they wrote about Lana's lovely blond coif and her magnificent wardrobe.

While Lana's flourishing career kept her busy, Cheryl was taking advantage of her grandmother. Like her daughter, Mildred enjoyed a few too many cocktails every night and fell into a deep sleep rather early. Cheryl began to sneak out of the house to meet her boyfriend but was caught in the act in January 1960. Lana and Crane rushed to Mildred's when they heard Cheryl was eloping. She changed her mind when Lana and Crane offered her a big church wedding and a lavish reception. It wasn't Cheryl's plans to elope that presented a big problem. It was her violating probation, and she was sent to El Retiro, a reform school in the San Fernando Valley. Cheryl managed to escape twice but was apprehended both times. Lana told the press that El Retiro was a place for "confused children" and she hoped Cheryl would "find herself" there.

Though she was not often seen in public with Fred May, Lana attended the Hollywood premiere of *Portrait in Black* with him on June 29, 1960. At a party at Romanoff's later, Fred May approached *Hollywood Reporter* gossip columnist Mike Connelly about some nasty remarks he had made about Lana and Cheryl. Fred grabbed Connelly by the tie and said, "I love this girl, and what you're writing about her is unfair." The two men were separated by other guests, but their verbal insults about each other continued. Lana's tears brought the fight to a halt. She later admired Fred for standing up to Connelly. Cheryl was grateful too, and she became very fond of May, who proved to be a loyal friend to the seventeen-year-old daughter of the woman he loved.

❋   ❋   ❋

In mid-1960 Lana was paid $300,000 and a percentage of
the profits for making *By Love Possessed* at United Artists.
She plays the alcoholic wife of Jason Robards, Jr., crippled
and impotent from an automobile accident. Lana has an
affair with her husband's law partner, Efrem Zimbalist, Jr.,
who eventually returns to his wife's bed.

By Love Possessed had all the elements of a soap opera
and, though not one of Lana's better films, she did not
disappoint her fans. A fine cast of players helped too.

In her private life, Lana was supported by Fred May,
the forty-three-year-old millionaire rancher, who was divorced and the father of two children. They took out a
marriage license in the summer of 1960 but didn't use it
until a day before it expired. On November 27, 1960, Lana
and Fred were married at the Miramar Hotel in Santa
Monica. "He's a wonderful guy," she said. "I wish I'd met
him years ago."

Lana gave up her residences in town and bought a
huge beach house in Malibu. She and Fred obtained a
working ranch in nearby Chino, where Mildred stayed to
help with the livestock. Cheryl was allowed to live in Malibu with Lana now that she was married to Fred May. But
Cheryl, running with a fast crowd, was arrested at a
drunken party on June 11. When Lana got a call from the
police station, she didn't have the strength to face the press,
so Fred brought his stepdaughter home. Though he pro-
tested, police said Cheryl had to report back the following
morning. Afraid that she would be returned to reform
school, Cheryl wrote her mother a note saying that she
needed to find herself, and then she vanished the same
night. A week later she answered newspaper appeals from
Lana and Crane to "please come home." Cheryl agreed,

but only if she did not have to go back to the reformatory. With only a month to go before her eighteenth birthday, she could think of little else than being free.

Lana, May, Crane, and Mildred sat down with Cheryl and quietly explained that she needed psychiatric help. It wasn't her fault, they said. Growing up in Hollywood was difficult, and because there were too many temptations, maybe it would be best if she could get away for counseling. Lana told her, "Fred and I will fly with you to the Institute for Living in Hartford, Conneticut. It's very much like a country club, dear."

The only disappointment Cheryl faced was not being released on her eighteenth birthday. She went into a rage and was put on a suicide watch. Her problems stemmed not only from knowing she could not leave until someone else signed her out but also from a doctor who insisted she talk about Johnny Stompanato. Another psychiatrist took over, and Cheryl settled down at the institute for almost a year.

While Lana was having her problems with Cheryl, she filmed *Bachelor in Paradise* with Bob Hope at MGM. He plays an author writing about "how Americans live." Doing his research while living in Paradise Village, Hope gets innocently involved (as only he can) with several house-wives and is taken to court by their husbands. During the trial he confesses his love for Lana, the only single woman living in Paradise.

Though she plays "straight man" to Hope, Lana is luscious, especially while doing a very sexy hula alone on the dance floor after a few drinks with Bob.

Lana then made another comedy, *Who's Got the Action?*, with Dean Martin cast as her horse-betting husband.

She decides to become his bookie to recoup his losses. Instead he goes on a winning streak and Lana has to hock everything to pay off his bets. Critics said everyone was a loser in this movie.

Lana was also a loser at marriage for the fifth time. Fred was becoming increasingly annoyed when she arrived home late from the studio. She explained that Dean Martin took long lunch hours, causing them to work overtime. But it went beyond that. If Lana was appearing in public, she fussed for hours. Fred was a punctual guy, and the arguments began. But he was also an understanding person, so these occasional annoyances did not break up the marriage.

In need of cash, Fred borrowed $18,000 from Lana. She took this in stride, but when he bought her a new Lincoln Continental with part of the money, Lana blew her stack. On the night of the argument, she fled in her new auto to a bar on the Pacific Coast Highway called the Cottage. She made a date with the bartender, parked the Lincoln in front of his apartment building, and threw her fur coat on his couch downstairs.

Worried about his wife, Fred May cruised the area and spotted her car. He peeked in the window, saw Lana's coat, and pounded on the front door. In a panic, she ran out the back door, wearing only her coat and dark glasses, and walked home on the beach.

As it happened, Mildred was passing by and saw her daughter's car and a very angry Fred May. She testified against Lana at the divorce hearing on October 15, 1962.

Before the "bartender" incident had appeared in *Confidential* magazine, Lana's friends tried to talk her into a reconciliation with Fred May. He was the most stable, patient, and sympathetic of all her husbands. But Lana was getting bored with the forever predictable Fred. She needed a more exciting man. Though she complained bitterly about being "pushed around" by Fernando Lamas and Bob Topping, Lana enjoyed the friction and the passion of making up. This time she didn't fret or go into a deep state of depression. Instead she went to Korea with Bob Hope to entertain the servicemen over the Christmas holidays. Though this might have been Lana's way of escaping newsmen, she found the tour very gratifying. "It was rewarding," she said. "It was exhausting, but all so worthwhile."

Lana remained friends with Fred May. He urged her to buy a Malibu house with ninety-five feet of beachfront. She took his advice and lived there for seven years. Lana and Fred saw each other frequently, and she continued to rely on him regarding personal matters, particularly if Cheryl was involved.

In October 1962, a novel by Harold Robbins entitled *Where Love Has Gone* became an instant best-seller. It was based loosely on the Stompanato case. In the book Lana is portrayed as a famous sculptress who stabs her lover and allows her daughter to take the blame. The novel had such an impact readers were convinced that it revealed the truth about Stompanato's death.

The Robbins book gained a good deal of publicity, and for Cheryl, it was reliving that dreadful night all over again. She was trying to make a new life for herself in Los Angeles, working as a carhop and doing other odd jobs under a different name in 1963. She began to drink heavily, became despondent, and took an overdose of sleeping pills. Fortunately, her roommate found Cheryl in time and rushed her to a hospital. During her recovery, she came to terms with herself and decided the time had come to put her life in order. She approached her father about working for him at his restaurant, the Luau. Elated, Crane gave her a job as a seater and began teaching his twenty-one-year-old daughter the business.

*   *   *

Lana next made *Love Has Many Faces* in Acapulco. The film's assets were primarily her fabulous outfits, designed by Edith Head. Playing a millionairess again, Lana is married to a former beach boy (Cliff Robertson), both of whom find life very dull. She plays with his young cronies and he finds solace with another woman (Stephanie Powers). When Lana is seriously injured in a fall from a horse, Robertson returns to nurse her back to health.

Press agent George Nichols said, "Lana was drinking during *Love Has Many Faces*. Acapulco reminded her of the past, the good and the bad times. It was difficult for me to believe Lana drank during working hours, but she did. Lana had flings, but she was very lonely . . . a frightened child. Alcohol gave her the confidence to face life every day."

Lana was not hurting for money, but her career was in a decline again. Good scripts were hard to find in Hollywood, and the former contract players did not want to lower themselves by appearing in trashy films.

In 1962 Lana and Ross Hunter had purchased the rights to *Madame X*, but script problems held up the production until 1965. In the film Lana portrays a young woman married to a wealthy diplomat (John Forsythe). Alone most of the time, she gets involved with another man, who dies in a freak accident. Fearing a scandal might ruin her husband's career, she leaves him and her son and is presumed dead. Her life from then on is a haze of alcohol and prostitution. In self-defense, she kills a man who threatens to reveal her identity and ruin her husband. Lana's defense attorney is her son, but before the trial is over she dies of a heart attack, and the young lawyer never finds out she is his mother.

Lana had to age twenty-four years in *Madame X*. As her character grew older in the film, Lana became depressed, spending more and more time with her makeup man. She and Ross Hunter clashed during production. Lana said he was angry because she took so long getting ready for the camera. But Hunter claimed Lana was staying up until all hours having a good time, and at forty-five, she could not expect to party all night and be fit to face the camera early the next morning.

Lana had meanwhile become involved with Robert Eaton, ten years younger, handsome, smooth, and divorced. His credentials? Aspiring actor/producer and stud. Lana said Eaton was the first man who satisfied her in bed, and she enjoyed the many stories about his sexual conquests. She told a friend they locked themselves in her bedroom for several days, making love. Maybe Lana's appetite for Eaton had something to do with her less-than-professional behavior on the set of *Madame X*. Sheila Graham hinted at this in one of her columns, writing that Constance Bennett, who played Lana's mother-in-law, looked younger *without* makeup than Lana did *with* makeup.

Eaton's outstanding qualification—that of a great love—was what Lana needed. In her mid-forties, she had found a man who could keep up with her in bed. As for Eaton, he had found a famous woman who could afford the expensive habits he was beginning to get used to. And so they were married on June 22, 1965, at his family's home in Arlington, Virginia.

Chapter 14

❋ MIRROR, MIRROR, ON THE WALL ❋

$\mathcal{L}$ANA HAD A FACE-LIFT IN 1966. IT WAS A guarded secret, of course, and the difference was barely noticeable. If one takes time to study pictures of her after the surgery, the eyes are slanted slightly and her "little girl" features have lost their lushness. But Lana was still the stunning and eternally beautiful screen legend.

There were movie projects that never got off the ground for Lana. As the saying goes, "The deals fell through." She did, however, appear on television. She sang a few tunes with Peter Lawford on "The Milton Berle Show," did a skit with Dinah Shore on the singer's weekly program, danced the bossa nova with Bob Hope on his 1963 Christmas show, spoofed it up with the Smothers Brothers, danced and did a comedy skit on "The Carol Burnett Show," and made several appearances on the popular "What's My Line?" as the mystery guest.

Lana's income from her movie projects with Ross Hunter had made her a millionaire, so she could afford to wait until another worthwhile film came along.

And she could afford to keep Bob Eaton dressed in expensive suits from the finest shops in Beverly Hills. Also, compliments of Lana, he had an operation on his "bum" eye to restore vision and his bad teeth were fixed. She bought Bob a car, gave him a monthly allowance, and set him up to oversee her Eltee Production company in a lavish office suite on Sunset Boulevard. However, Eaton preferred using Lana's Malibu house for entertaining clients. Annoyed by the endless parties but determined to let her husband have his own way, Lana went to Vietnam on a USO tour in June 1967. Though she sprained her ankle and had to use a wheelchair, Lana did not cancel any of her scheduled appearances at American bases and hospitals.

Three weeks later she returned home. Wildly enthusiastic about her trip into the jungles of Vietnam, she paid little attention to the gossip about Eaton's nightclub sprees. Finally, Mildred told Lana that Bob had "entertained" other women at the Malibu house and that she'd kept the stained sheets to prove it. The evidence was bad enough, but knowing Eaton had used their bed for his trysts was unforgivable. Lana confronted Bob and he turned as white as the sheets. She told him to pack his things and get out. She filed for divorce, but they reconciled.

The Big Cube, filmed in Acapulco and financed by ANCO, a Mexican firm, was a Lana Turner embarrassment. She played a rich widow whose stepdaughter tries to drive her insane by lacing Lana's food with LSD. *The Big Cube* did well in Mexico, but it was released only in neighborhood theaters in America and soon forgotten.

Lana put this disaster behind her and concentrated on a television series that Eaton was working on for her. When she found out "The Survivors" was a Harold Robbins project, Lana was skeptical about working with the author of *Where Love Has Gone* based, supposedly on the Stompanato affair. When Eaton introduced Lana to Robbins, she gave the author a limp handshake and kept her distance. But a good TV project was almost as difficult to find as a worthwhile movie script.

Lana signed on to do "The Survivors." ABC-Universal announced the forthcoming series at a celebration party at the Bistro in Hollywood. Other members of the cast included Kevin McCarthy, Ralph Bellamy, and George Hamilton.

In early 1968, Lana, Eaton, and the production company went to the Riviera to shoot exterior scenes. Trouble started when the producer, William Frye, and Lana got into a heated argument. She slapped him, he slapped her back, and Frye was fired. Lana called Universal executive Grant Tinker, who took over temporarily.

Bob Eaton contributed very little to his wife's television series while they were abroad. But he felt duty-bound to go after Frye for slapping his wife. Both men got in one punch and that was the extent of Eaton's show of gallantry. Perhaps he needed to defend her honor since he'd been playing around while Lana worked. But she knew what Bob was up to and told him to get out of her Malibu house. She filed for divorce in April 1968.

Lana kept busy working on interior scenes for "The Survivors." The series revolved around Tracy Hastings, played by Lana; her philandering husband, Philip (Kevin McCarthy); her banking czar father (Ralph Bellamy); and a playboy half-brother (George Hamilton). The Hastings' only child, Jeffrey (Jan-Michael Vincent) was actually the son of Tracy's lover Antaeus Riakos (Rossano Brazzi).

After two years of planning, script revisions, and postponements, the TV series made its debut on September 29, 1969, but the show lasted only fifteen weeks.

Lana said she had no idea what was happening from one episode to another. She didn't know what Tracy Hastings was all about, what made her tick. About the cast she said, "In the beginning we hated each other. At the end we simply disliked each other."

Lana's salary was $12,000 per episode, while George Hamilton made $17,000. She said it was a matter of top billing or the money, and MGM had taught her that top billing was more prestigious than the almighty buck. Actually the top billing *was* more prestigious, but the sponsors thought George Hamilton would attract more viewers. They were wrong and the show was canceled. Lana wept privately, but not for the obvious reasons. She missed reporting to the set every day, joking with technicians, and chatting with old friends working on other TV shows. It was like old times at MGM.

Before "The Survivors" was launched on ABC, Lana sold her house in Malibu and rented another on Coldwater Canyon Drive in Beverly Hills. Though her film career had come to a halt, there were many offers to guest-star on TV shows in New York. Her social life left a good deal to be desired, and though Lana was lonely without a husband to come home to, she wondered if there was a man alive who would not let her down.

In April 1969, shortly after her divorce from Bob Eaton became final, Lana was at a popular disco called The Candy Store when a tall gentleman asked her to dance. She accepted because, as she said in her autobiography, she'd spotted Bob "standing at the bar with a striking brunette." Lana said the stranger was handsome, but Ronald Dante's "frog" eyes and gaunt face made him less than attractive. It was so dark in the disco that Dante, for his part, didn't realize the lovely blonde was Lana Turner. When she found out he was a nightclub hypnotist, Lana wanted to know if he could help her stop smoking. Dante didn't make any promises, but they exchanged telephone numbers. He called a few days later and made a date with Lana. She was taken aback when Dante showed up with his motorcycle and offered her a ride. Without hesitation, Lana got on behind him and wrapped her arms tightly around his waist. Speeding through the hills of Hollywood was a thrill for Lana, who had experienced just about everything else in her lifetime.

Dante, who claimed to be forty-nine years old, told Lana he'd been born in Singapore, where he earned his college degree in psychology. She said it was love at first sight, and friends wondered if Dante had hypnotized Lana into believing it. He proposed almost immediately, and when she turned him down, he stopped calling. Lana knew this was an old trick, but loneliness got the best of her, and when Dante phoned again she had a change of heart. They were married in Las Vegas on May 9, 1969, less than six weeks after Lana's divorce from Bob Eaton was final.

The press wasted no time checking into Ronald Dante's background. His real name was Ronald Peller and he was born in Chicago in 1930. Supposedly he'd swindled one of his previous wives out of her life's savings. She sued for an annulment in 1963, claiming Peller had hypnotized her into getting married. She wanted her money back and the judge ruled in her favor.

Not long after Dante married Lana, he claimed that a man wearing an Australian bush hat shot at him while he was parking in an underground garage in West Hollywood. Dante told police he escaped injury by falling to the floor of his car. He said he had no idea why anyone would want to kill him, and the gunman was never found. When Lana heard about the incident, she fainted.

Many suspected Dante was looking for publicity. If so

it backfired, because Santa Ana police had been looking for him on a grand theft felony charge for a year. Supposedly he'd issued a bad check for $18,000. Dante had been arrested, posted $12,500 bail, and then disappeared. After the shooting incident, Dante told police that his life had been threatened and he suspected those to whom he owed the remainder of the debt. The theft charges were eventually dropped.

It's not known if Lana used her influence in Dante's behalf, but she surely proved her desire to do anything for him during their marriage. Lana went out of her way to be with Dante at his out-of-town nightclub engagements. When word got around that Lana Turner would be in attendance, larger audiences showed up to see Dante, magician and hypnotist, and his famous wife. He would introduce Lana and she'd take a bow, waving to the crowd. But working on "The Survivors" and traveling with Dante was draining her energy, and in November 1969 Lana gave him a check for $35,000 to invest in a business that would keep him at home. This financial transaction transpired the day before a trip to San Francisco, where Lana was scheduled to appear at a benefit for the Presbyterian Children's Hospital. Accompanying Lana were Dante, her new secretary, Taylor Pero, and public-relations representative Phil Sinclair.

Lana avoided public appearances, aside from the brief ones on behalf of Dante. She was very sensitive about approaching fifty, knowing that observant fans were comparing her face and figure to the luscious screen star of the forties and fifties.

Lana relied on vodka to ease the pain of these ordeals, but she rarely showed the effects of drinking. The charity event in San Francisco was an exception. During the dinner dance at the Museum of Natural History in Golden Gate

Park, Lana, wearing a stunning red lace gown, mingled with Dante at her side. When she appeared on stage, however, she slurred her words. If that wasn't bad enough, Lana decided to sing "I Left My Heart in San Francisco." Vocalizing was not one of Lana's talents. Then she forgot the words and motioned to Taylor Pero, who finished the number with her. (Pero had previously worked with Johnny Mathis as a singer and dancer. He'd also handled press and public relations for Mathis.)

After the benefit, Lana made the round of nightclubs with Dante, Sinclair, and Pero. She voluntarily went up on stage at Finocchio's to dance with the transvestites, and at the Casa Madrid she did a wild flamenco. No liquor was served after 2:00 A.M., so Lana suggested they return to her posh suite at the Mark Hopkins Hotel for more drinks. On the way she wanted something to eat, but Sinclair advised her not to stop anywhere because she was dripping with diamonds. He offered to get some food after dropping her off at the hotel, and Dante said he'd tag along.

Less than an hour later Sinclair returned to the hotel alone. He said Dante had gotten out of the limousine without explanation and hailed a cab. Lana sat up all night waiting for a call from her husband—a call that never came. She decided to see the sights in San Francisco with Pero the next day after only a few hours' sleep. Not having heard from Dante, Lana returned home that night to discover that his motorcycle and clothes were gone. He'd left her a note saying he needed to be on his own. Lana read it and fainted. When she came around, Pero reminded her about the $35,000 check she had given to him on Friday. Lana put a stop on the check, which she referred to as a "loan."

The next day, a Monday, news leaked out to the newspapers that Dante had deserted Lana. Humilated, she went to work anyway. Everyone on the set of "The Survivors" went about their business as if nothing had happened. But it wasn't long before Lana had to face another disappointment. Her TV series had been canceled. She demanded full payment according to her contract and got it. She also took her wardrobe without asking, because this too was part of the agreement.

She relied on Taylor Pero for consolation and company. At her request, he moved into her guest room and was Lana's frequent escort.

In December 1969, Lana sued Dante for divorce and accused him of fraud. He, in turn, wanted $250,000. It would take three years before the case was settled in Lana's favor, except she never got her $35,000 back. "I'm so gullible," she said. "I always thought I was being loved for myself."

In February 1970 Lana's interior decorator, Vince Pastere, invited her to spend a week at his house in Palm Springs. There Lana received a phone call from Dante, who said he missed her and hoped they could remain friends. She wasn't prepared for this call in the middle of the night, nor the romantic one-way conversation. Dante wanted to know how long she would be in Palm Springs, and she replied, "Two or three more days." He told her to have a wonderful time and hung up.

When Lana and Taylor Pero returned home, they noticed the sliding-glass doors to the swimming pool were open. While they waited for the police, Lana discovered that $100,000 worth of jewelry was missing. The thief and missing jewelry were never found.

Lana felt it was time to move again. As before, the house had only unhappy memories for her. Because of the robbery, she chose a penthouse apartment at the Edgewater Towers, overlooking the Pacific. This was not an easy adjustment for Lana, who liked the spaciousness of her house in Coldwater Canyon with its white marble fireplace and floors, white carpeting, and landscaping.

Though Pero did his work at Lana's place, he did not feel the need to stay with her now that she had the protection of a doorman and security guards. But Lana was possessive if she was fond of a man, and Taylor Pero was a very handsome thirty-year-old fellow. His charm and patience were invaluable to Lana. He could handle himself on all occasions—at a dinner party at Frank Sinatra's or at formal gatherings that required good manners, tact, and diplomacy. With her growing dependence on Pero, Lana resented his singing engagements and anyone or anything else that took him away from her. Though Lana denied this, Pero claimed he became intimate with Lana in early 1970 and he began spending more time with her.

After Lana was settled in her new apartment, she and Pero spent a month in Hawaii. This carefree life would impress most people, but she had mixed feelings about it. Though Lana didn't need the money, she still wanted to work but there were few offers coming her way. While many stars of the Golden Era were turning down scripts, she was overlooked because of her fetish for glamorous roles. Lana was so vain about her looks that, several years before, during the filming of *Madame X*, she wore a veil to and from her dressing room and the set, which was closed.

In 1971 Lana was approached about appearing on stage in *Forty Carats*, and her immediate reaction was negative. She had never performed before a live audience, and the mere thought of it terrified her. By comparison, making movies was easy. If she forgot her lines, there were retakes. Not so in the theater. Producers Shelley Gross and Lee Guber offered Lana $17,500 a week, coaxing her to reconsider. She was promised the best accommodations, a luxurious wardrobe, and her own hairdresser and makeup staff. But Lana wasn't satisfied. Director John Bowab had been highly recommended to her, and she told Gross and Guber that if they could get Bowab they had a deal. Lana got her way.

Nolan Miller designed fourteen magnificent outfits for Lana and two fabulous gowns for her curtain calls. She relied on Pero, who worked with Lana diligently on her lines. In *Forty Carats* she played a forty-year-old divorcée in love with a man half her age, a role that was perfect for Lana.

Preparations were going along smoothly until shortly before she was scheduled for rehearsals in New York. Lana was drinking more than usual to calm her nerves and taking Seconals to help her sleep. During the night she would occasionally call friends, who were disturbed by her incoherence and slurred voice. On one occasion Lana mumbled on the telephone that she could not go through with the play, and a close acquaintance called an ambulance. Lana was embarrassed that medics found her in a disheveled state, sans eyebrows. Her life was not in danger, nor did Lana attempt suicide. As was the habit of her peers Judy Garland and Marilyn Monroe, Lana was reaching out for reassurance and attention.

In May 1971 Lana flew to New York. She stayed at the Plaza Hotel, which was only a few blocks from the rehearsal hall, but she expected a limousine nonetheless. Her request was politely ignored by director Bowab, who put his arm around Lana and said the fresh air and exercise would do her good. She was outraged by this indignity. At MGM she had a limousine to take her across the street! Joan Crawford's chauffeur was always waiting to drive the actress from her dressing room to the MGM photo studio a few doors away.

Lana would have to make other adjustments that today's players find impossible to believe. During the Golden Era, one did not walk up to the great stars without a proper introduction. It was unthinkable to touch them unless your Hollywood status was the same or you were a very close friend. These stars were approached with reverence and referred to as "Miss Turner," or "Mr. Gable."

At Lana's first stage rehearsal in New York she was greeted respectfully, but within the hour members of the cast were treating her like one of the family. At first Lana was offended, but the sincerity of their friendliness soon put her at ease.

Columnist Earl Wilson met Lana and Pero for lunch at the Russian Tea Room. They all had cocktails while she puffed away on little brown Sherman cigars, one after the other. Nibbling on smoked salmon and capers, Lana told Wilson, "When I got the call about *Forty Carats* I assumed it was the movie, but I was tired of sitting around. I thought doing a play would be a challenge."

"Have you seen Artie?" Wilson asked.

"Artie who?" Lana said with a smile.

"Are you going to get married again?"

"You didn't ask me that, did you? Because I didn't hear you."

Wilson got the message and asked about the play. Lana perked up and replied, "We open in Sandy Grove, Maryland, on June 8 and then the Westbury Music Fair June 29. We play in-the-round with all those ramps. I've never done a proscenium show. Why, I've never even done a high-school play!"

Lana was on the road with *Forty Carats* for ten weeks. The reviews were mild. Many critics complained that Lana was merely playing Lana Turner, while other critics were delighted to see Lana "portray" herself. Then there was her quick change into a glittering bow gown while the audiences were preparing to leave the theater. To some critics it was corny and pretentious. To others it was class and glamour personified. Lana's attitude was that the public had come to see an MGM star and, by God, they were going to have the opportunity to see the glamorous actress as she had appeared on the screen.

Chapter 15

✳ CLINGING TO YESTERDAY ✳

$\mathcal{L}$ANA WAS EXHAUSTED AFTER TOURING IN *Forty Carats*. She would laze about watching television, sipping vodka, and sleeping until the afternoon. Occasionally, she saw Cheryl, who was living with Joyce "Josh" LeRoy. In their late twenties, both girls had known for some time that they preferred women, but it was difficult in 1970 to face this truth. Cheryl and Josh are still together as of this writing.

Mildred, who was approaching seventy, moved in with the girls and thought nothing of the relationship. She was more broad-minded than Lana. It would take Cheryl's mother a few years to accept her daughter's way of life. Concerned only about herself in the 1970s, Lana did not take the time to sit down with her daughter and talk things out. Had they done so, she might have been indebted to Josh for helping Cheryl put the memories of a lonely and unhappy childhood in the past, where they belonged. By contrast, Lana clung to her glamorous yesterdays at MGM and the all-important "clean" image of perfection that ruled out homosexuality in the family. According to a close friend, Lana blamed herself that Cheryl was gay: "She felt guilty for not taking more interest in her daughter. There was Lex Barker's abuse that happened right under her nose. Lana couldn't pinpoint her mistakes because she'd made a lot of them where Cheryl was concerned. She'd been divorced seven times and then there was her passion for Johnny Stompanato that ultimately changed Cheryl's life forever. As long as Lana perched herself on a pedestal, she was out of touch with the outside world of reality."

In March 1972 Lana was asked to endorse a chain of health spas. Following two months of negotiations, the Lana Turner Minispas opened around the country. She did "The Mike Douglas Show" on television and enjoyed a lengthy interview with David Frost to promote the health centers. But her appearance on Johnny Carson's "Tonight Show" went badly. Lana talked about her newly sponsored spas, but Johnny got off the subject by mentioning her reputation for being temperamental. Lana said she was aware of it and smiled as if to say "Shall we talk about something else?" Johnny continued to tease her and, sensing Lana's annoyance, suggested she get it out of her system. Throw an ashtray, perhaps. Again Lana ignored his rudeness, so Johnny picked up the ashtray and threw it over his shoulder. He grinned, Ed McMahon grinned, and Lana stood up, thanked Johnny, and waved to the audience as she walked off the set. So much for the Carson show and so much for the Lana Turner Minispas, which folded in the fall of 1972.

After four years off the screen, Lana signed for the lead in *I Hate You, Cat*, a horror movie to be filmed in London.

She should have turned down the project, but Lana couldn't ignore the success of a similar film, *What Ever Happened to Baby Jane?*, with Joan Crawford and Bette Davis, who was nominated for an Oscar in 1962. Olivia de Havilland and Joseph Cotten joined Davis in *Hush . . . Hush, Sweet Charlotte*, (1965), a macabre film that was also successful at the box office. Barbara Stanwyck co-starred with her ex-husband Robert Taylor in *The Night Walker* (1964), another horror thriller.

Lana finally decided to join these illustrious players who were adjusting to the new trend in Hollywood. Her only quarrel with *I Hate You, Cat* was the title. It was changed to *The Terror of Sheba* but would be released as *Persecution*. Lana plays a deranged mother who gets revenge on her son for drowning her favorite cat Sheba in its milk. Lana has many cats named Sheba in the film, and she uses them to drive her son and his wife mad. At the end he drowns his mother in Sheba's milk.

Before Lana left for England to make this atrocious film, she bought a condominium at Century Park East on Santa Monica Boulevard in Century City. Though her apartment at the Edgewater was bigger, the building had been neglected and was going co-op. Lana was contented at Century City East, with its magnificent view and convenient location. She would not move again.

After a year's delay, Lana and Pero flew to London for *Persecution* in October 1973. She told the British press, "This is entirely different from anything I've ever done before. I'm sure I'll get a lot of hate mail." Only a few theaters in the United States showed *Persecution*, and the British critics were disappointed in the film. But they thought Lana looked spectacular, and to her amazement she won the Silver Carnation for best actress at the Sitges Festival of Horror films in Spain.

The year 1974 was an uneventful one for Lana. She had a few stage and screen offers but deemed them unsuitable for a star of her stature. Not that Lana didn't agree to discuss these projects. She did, but her demands for script revisions were rejected. She would play an adulteress, a murderer, and a mother, but Lana refused any part that did not reflect her famous blonde image. She had another face-lift and remained dedicated to looking her very best. Even if Lana did not go out, her hairdresser and manicurist came to the apartment every week.

In the spring of 1975 Lana was asked to attend a tribute in her honor at Town Hall in New York. She was terrified at the mere thought but knew it would generate the kind of publicity she needed. Two thousand people showed up at Town Hall on April 13 to see the one and only Lana. She did not show up for her film clips as the majority of honorees did. Instead, Lana kept the audience in anticipation until it was time for her appearance on stage.

In keeping with her tenure at MGM, Lana's press interviews were fluffy and pure. She emphasized her pride in Cheryl and how close they were. As for romance, Lana said she had been celibate since 1969. When asked about Taylor Pero, who was always with her, Lana said he was her secretary and nothing more. The very idea that they were lovers was absurd.

But the many people who saw Lana and Pero together had no doubts about an intimate relationship. Though they did not display any affection in public, an observer said,

"Pero was remarkably handsome. Stunning, in fact. He attracted women but rarely strayed from Lana's side. Nothing unusual in Hollywood for an aging actress to have a young stud. Lana flaunted him, in a way, and could not conceal her jealousy if he talked to other women at parties. Pero got the short end of the stick because I know she wasn't supporting him."

In November 1975, Lana appeared on stage in *The Pleasure of His Company* for three weeks in Arlington Heights, Illinois. She and Louis Jourdan played a divorced couple who are reunited at their daughter's wedding. Lana insisted that John Bowab direct the play, which was such a success it was held over for a month. *The Pleasure of His Company* might have continued for another few weeks if Jourdan did not have another commitment. Lana refused to perform with an unknown, but rather than admit the truth, she managed to get sick and returned to Los Angeles.

Lana faced a health crisis in early 1976. During a routine physical examination, her doctor suspected cancer of the cervix. She was treated at the Southern California Cancer Center and within weeks the symptoms disappeared. Lana used an assumed name and wore a black wig when she went to the cancer center. Fearing the worst, Lana cut back on vodka and cigarettes, but when the crisis had passed, she resumed drinking and smoking.

In the summer of 1976, Lana went on tour for ten weeks in *Bell, Book and Candle*. The play was very successful, and Lana received rave reviews. She would not, however, perform if there were many empty seats in the theater. Fortunately, this was a rare occurrence.

Following *Bell, Book, and Candle*, Lana accepted an offer from Avco Embassy Pictures to film *Bittersweet Love*, the story about newlyweds who discover they have the same father. Lana portrayed the mother of the doomed bride, played by Meredith Baxter-Birney. Despite a cast that included Robert Alda, Celeste Holm, and Robert Lansing, the movie was a flop. Lana said *Bittersweet Love* did not do well because it wasn't publicized. Like *Persecution*, the film was shown only in neighborhood theaters and disappeared.

In 1977 Lana was hospitalized with a liver ailment. When she recovered, doctors told her to give up drinking or suffer the consequences. Lana obeyed orders for as long as she could stand it. Instead of tonic, she drank vodka with cranberry juice. When close friends discovered her secret, they expressed concern. Lana retorted that it was the only way she could face the day, particularly during interviews or negotiations for projects that usually did not materialize. If they did come through, she couldn't face an audience or camera without vodka.

In 1978 Lana filmed *Witches Brew*, with Teri Garr and Richard Benjamin, but the movie was never released due to legal entanglements involving producer Jack Bean. Before Lana received the bad news, she was asked to do another play, *Divorce Me, Darling*, in Chicago. Word quickly got around that Lana Turner had become a first-rate stage actress, and she eagerly toured in *Murder Among Friends* for Tony De Santis at his Drury Lane Theatre. The ultimate plan was for Lana to appear on Broadway in the play. She was superb as a woman planning to kill her husband with the help of her boyfriend, who is also the husband's lover.

But Lana's success went to her head when *Murder Among Friends* was playing in Chicago. She began arriving later and later, until audiences either booed or left the theater demanding their money back. Taylor Pero couldn't handle her, nor could anyone else who was connected with the play. But audiences quickly forgave Lana when she made her first entrance on stage. That she was greeted with applause after delaying the curtain for over an hour seemed to give Lana a good deal of pleasure after getting dirty looks backstage. She got away with it in Chicago, but Broadway wanted no part of Lana. So what? She didn't want to live in New York anyway.

Phil Sinclair, who had been in San Francisco with Lana when Dante disappeared, came up with an idea to do a series of tributes to Lana Turner in San Francisco, Miami, New Orleans, Washington, D.C., and Atlanta. With nothing else on the horizon, Lana was delighted. Pero wasn't sure he wanted any part of getting her anywhere on time again, but Lana seemed lost without him and he reluctantly agreed to go along.

On November 5, 1978, Lana arrived two hours late at the Warfield Theatre in San Francisco. Though she was the honored guest, the proceeds from these tributes went to Lana's favorite charity, "Bean Sprouts," a television series to benefit Chinese-American children. Her tardiness, therefore, was an insult not only to those persons involved with the charity but to the contributors as well. Once again Lana charmed the audience, even though she slithered down the aisle during the showing of her film clips. She got a standing ovation. Later, at a gala reception for several hundred people, Lana mingled with the guests, who forgot she'd kept them waiting, but only a few reporters had the patience to hang around. Without good press coverage, "Bean Sprouts" was the loser.

In New Orleans, not many people showed up at Lana's charity tribute. Miami was worse. Lana blamed the small ticket sales on lack of publicity. What she failed to understand was that her demands for traveling first-class were depleting the meager profits.

Claiming she was ill, Lana refused to attend the Miami benefit. The sponsors sent a physician to the hotel for verification that Lana was really sick, and she somehow managed to con the starstruck doctor. Phil Sinclair canceled the Washington, D.C., tribute for fear of offending Senator John Warner and his wife, Elizabeth Taylor. Lana wanted to forget Atlanta and return to Los Angeles, but Sinclair told her that advance ticket sales in Georgia were very good. Unfortunately, news of Lana's no-show in Miami had reached Atlanta and its World Congress Center was half empty.

The stress of the tour and Lana's bad temperament caused another rift between her and Taylor Pero. They had a bitter fight, and she fired him in November 1979. Alone again, Lana flew to Hawaii to spend Thanksgiving with Cheryl, who had settled in Honolulu with Josh. Nervous and argumentative, Lana cut short her visit.

In the spring of 1980, Lana decided to write her memoirs when she found out that Pero was writing a book titled *Always Lana* about their ten years together. She received a good deal of publicity by appearing on major TV talk shows. Lana said she had found God, had given up drinking, and had been celibate since 1969.

Lana: The Lady, the Legend, the Truth was a bestseller in 1982. Indeed, Lana was always the lady and would always be a legend, but Hollywood columnists who had been around a long time got a chuckle over Lana's emphasizing "the truth" in her title. Sheila Graham said, "When a Hollywood queen claims she's telling the truth and nothing but the truth, she's hiding 'behind' the truth."

Pero's *Always Lana* (1982) was more interesting, even though he wrote about his former boss with great compassion. He kept Lana on a throne but removed her crown when the occasion warranted and handled their intimacy with discretion, emphasizing the good times they'd had together and the disappointments they shared. Pero said he wanted to marry Lana and was devastated when they parted, but he would not beg for his job back. Though Lana wrote very little about Taylor Pero in her memoirs, other than to deny they were lovers, she fell apart after they went their separate ways. Her weight dropped to under a hundred pounds, and admittedly she was drinking heavily and not eating. At the advice of a close friend, Lana turned to holistic medicine and pulled herself together. "When you accept God, you're never alone," she said.

Cheryl made another attempt at reconciling with her mother and invited Lana to Hawaii. It was not a movie goddess who stepped off the airplane this time, rather a woman who wore casual clothes and little makeup. They talked candidly, settled their differences, and understood each other at long last. Lana embraced Josh as a daughter, perhaps the dearest gift that Cheryl could ask for. "Though I grew up before my mother did, she caught up," Cheryl wrote in her book, *Detour.*

On February 22, 1982, Mildred, who suffered from emphysema, died in Hawaii. She and Lana were close in the final years and together at the end. Cheryl had convinced her mother to buy a house in Hawaii so they could be together several months a year. Lana walked around the island without being recognized for the most part. When she was approached by a fan, she was casual and chatty.

In October Lana embarked on a tour to promote her book. Reporters noted that she did not travel with trunks of gowns and furs or a jewelry case filled with her famous emeralds and diamonds. "I'm an author," she said, "traveling with two suitcases and two garment bags." Her companions on the tour were her devoted maid, Carmen, and her good-looking hairdresser, Eric Root.

"The public has been warm," Lana told Arthur Bell of *The Village Voice.* "I've been blessed." She mentioned that her marriage to Fred May was the happiest. "He's married now to a gal I adore and she likes me. We're still friends. He helps me with my business affairs." As for husband number seven, who she believes robbed her of $100,000 in jewelry, Lana said, "That bastard. Ronald Dante, he called himself. I never did now what his real name was. That schmuck." Then Lana laughed uproariously according to Arthur Bell, who commented that no one ever captured the feisty side of Lana's personality on film.

"They don't know I'm really 'Auntie Mame,' " she said. "They haven't tapped my roots!"

Lana was adamant that she would not discuss Johnny Stompanato, her husbands, Tyrone Power, or her leading men during TV interviews. When asked about sex, Lana said she was celibate and had been for several years. "Frankly, I don't want a physical relationship," she said. "Sex doesn't mean that much to me. It never did."

Lana retired from show business in 1983 after appearing in the prime-time soap opera "Falcon Crest."

The following year Robin Leach asked her to be on his popular weekly television show, "Lifestyles of the Rich and Famous." Lana agreed to appear if her segments were filmed in Egypt—all expenses paid, of course. While she was boarding a plane in Los Angeles on the first trek of her long journey, Lana stumbled on a staircase leading to the plane as fans scrambled for her autograph. When she arrived at New York's Kennedy Airport, Lana was wheeled off the jet in excruciating pain from a sprained ankle.

Robin Leach told reporters he was very distraught and wondered if Lana would be able to make the trip. "I've already spent a fortune," he said. "I don't know what's going to happen."

Lana and her hairdresser, Eric Root, went into seclusion at a Midtown hotel and refused to take any calls. But two days later, on April 24, 1984, she boarded the plane for Cairo with Root and Leach.

Sitting on a gilded chair that resembled a throne, Lana told Leach that her trip to Egypt was a sentimental journey to a land that she mysteriously felt she already knew. "I've been here in a past life," she said. "I don't know how many thousands of years ago, and I keep feeling a fulfillment coming. I believe in reincarnation. There's a very deep spiritual reason for me to be here in Cairo this very minute as we speak."

With the Sphinx and Giza pyramids in the background, Lana and Eric Root took a camel ride in the desert. He was obviously comfortable on the decorated beast, but Lana appeared to be enduring it for the camera's sake. On a cruise down the Nile she was filmed dancing with her hairdresser, but once again it was obvious she was not comfortable despite Root's guidance.

* * *

"Looking back on your life, are you at the happiest point of it all?" Leach asked.

"Oh, yes," Lana said with a sigh. "I have a glorious life. I can do anything I want, go where I want, be alone if I want, travel if I want, and sometimes I don't want anything. Now isn't that a blessing?"

Chapter 16

✳ SECLUSION ✳

WHEN CHERYL'S FATHER, STEPHAN CRANE, became ill in 1985, she and Josh moved to San Francisco. Crane, who'd made millions in the restaurant business, had had many beautiful girlfriends and five wives. Though he never said so, close friends believe that Lana was his greatest love. Crane spent the last few months of his life drinking alone and died from cirrhosis in February 1985.

Lana, too, preferred her privacy. Unlike her MGM sisters Cyd Charisse, Jane Powell, June Allyson, Esther Williams, Angela Lansbury, and Katharine Hepburn, Lana told friends, "I don't want people looking at me, saying, 'What's happened to her? God, she's old!' I want my fans to remember me as I was."

Cheryl was concerned about Lana when she decided to write her own autobiography, titled *Detour*, in 1988. They talked it over and Lana encouraged her to tell the truth about Josh, Lex Barker's sexual abuse, Johnny Stompanato's death, and her troubled childhood. The book was a hugh success. Cheryl appeared on TV talk shows, sometimes with Josh.

* * *

In June 1992, it was reported that Lana was taking treatments for throat cancer, which was spreading to her jaw and lungs. Lana had been bothered with a sore throat for months, and Cheryl insisted her mother check into Cedars-Sinai Medical Center on May 13 for a battery of tests. Lana vowed to survive this setback, but doctors confirmed it would be an uphill battle. Despite the prognosis, Lana beat the odds. On her birthday, February 8, 1993, she told friends in a hoarse voice that she was completely recovered. One gossip columnist wrote, "The blond movie queen retained her royal status during radiation therapy. Instead of a hospital gown, she wore an off-the-shoulder peasant blouse."

Because Lana had chosen a reclusive life, her friends were sure she would never appear in public again after her illness, but Lana emerged at the premiere of *Sunset Boulevard* in Los Angeles with Cheryl in December 1993. Lovely in a black sequin gown, Lana allowed photographers to take pictures. Those who spoke with her that night said she could barely talk. In private she resorted to writing everything down on paper. Lana was hospitalized again in the winter of 1994 with a mild case of pneumonia. She was released reportedly in good health.

To understand the girl who was tagged the Sweater Girl during the Golden Era of films is to understand the MGM family and its father, Louis B. Mayer. This studio that boasted it had more stars than there are in Heaven was the gem of Hollywood—a fourteen-karat blend of Cartier's and

Tiffany's, the finest finishing school in the world. The greatest raw talent was molded at Metro-Goldwyn-Mayer, and Louis B. Mayer made sure his creations were one of a kind. Lana Turner was one of his best.

Lana's former secretary, Taylor Pero, wrote in his book, *Always, Lana,* "Image before truth, facade rather than fact, pride over all—that was Louis B. Mayer's and Hollywood's legacy to Lana Turner." Pero spoke to actress Bette Davis about the star system. She told him, "My basic interest was the performance, not the off-screen image. Lana was different. She consciously perpetuated the glamour thing." Davis said she felt no obligation to anyone when she wasn't working, until her peers in Hollywood convinced her that an off-screen impression was just as important. "That's how you come to be preoccupied with your appearance. I realized I owed the public something. People like Lana never appeared in public any way but put together. I think the public still wants that. There's nothing to copy about an actress's hair or makeup or dress anymore. Look the way you want to at home, live your own life, but give the American people their kings and queens."

Taylor Pero told this author, "Dear Lana, selflessly saving Hollywood from decline!"

As for Lana's acting, director Vincent Minnelli said, "She was capable of brilliant individual scenes but seemed to lack the temperament or the training to sustain a full-length performance."

Hollywood historian David Shipman wrote, "Lana Turner has no other identity than that of a film star—and that from a mold, a fabulous creature who moves on-screen among beautiful furnishings, and who, off-screen, is primarily noted for a series of love affairs and marriages. It is presumably due to this that she owes the longevity of her career, which has consistently triumphed over appalling personal notices. Even her admirers would admit that she couldn't act her way out of a paper bag."

This author disagrees with friend Shipman. Lana Turner's career in films lasted *despite* her personal mishaps. Moviegoers paid to see a screen personality, not a great actress. Men came to feast their eyes and women to emulate perfection.

Lana Turner will be remembered as a beautiful, vibrant woman who lived life with the zest and passion that novelists attempt to emulate in fiction. She is a movie legend who would almost have us believe that the chiffon and tinsel still exist in Hollywood.

A STAR IS BORN

(David O. Selznick for United Artists, 1937)
Director: William A. Wellman
Producer: David O. Selznick
Screenplay: Dorothy Parker, from a story by William A. Wellman and Robert Carson
Cast: Janet Gaynor, Fredric March, Adolph Menjou, May Robson, Andy Devine; Lana worked as an extra
111 minutes

THEY WON'T FORGET

(A First National Picture for Warner Brothers, 1937)
Producer and Director: Mervyn LeRoy
Screenplay: Robert Rossen and Aben Kandel, from the novel *Death in the Deep South*, by Ward Greene
Photography: Arthur Edeson
Editor: Thomas Richards
Cast: Claude Rains, Gloria Dickson, Edward Norris, Otto Kruger, Allyn Joslyn, Lana Turner
95 minutes

✳ ✳ ✳

THE GREAT GARRICK

(Warner Brothers, 1937)

Director: James Whale

Screenplay: Ernst Vajda, based on "Ladies and Gentlemen," a story by Ernst Vajda

Photography: Ernest Haller

Editor: Warren Low

Cast: Brian Aherne, Olivia de Havilland, Edward Everett
Horton, Melville Cooper, Lionel Atwill, Luis Alverni,
Lana Turner, Marie Wilson

89 minutes

THE ADVENTURES OF MARCO POLO

(A Samuel Goldwyn Production for United Artists, 1938)

Director: Archie Mayo

Producer: Samuel Goldwyn

Screenplay: Robert E. Sherwood, from the story by N. A.
Pogson

Photography: Rudolph Mate

Editor: Fred Allen

Cast: Gary Cooper, Sigrid Gurie, Basil Rathbone, Ernest
Truex, Alan Hale, George Barbier, Binnie Barnes,
Lana Turner, Stanley Fields

104 minutes

LOVE FINDS ANDY HARDY

(MGM, 1938)

Director: George B. Seitz

Producer: Carey Wilson

Screenplay: William Ludwig, from the stories by Vivien
R. Bretherton and based on characters created by Au-
rania Rouverol

Cast: Lewis Stone, Mickey Rooney, Judy Garland, Cecilia Parker, Fay Holden, Lana Turner
91 minutes

THE CHASER

(*MGM, 1938*)
Director: Edwin L. Marin
Producer: Frank Davis
Screenplay: Everett Freeman, Harry Ruskin, and Bella and Sam Spewack, from an original story by Chandler Sprague and Howard Emmett Rogers
Photography: Charles Lawton, Jr.
Editor: George Boemler
Cast: Dennis O'Keefe, Ann Morriss, Lewis Stone, Nat Pendleton, Henry O'Neill, Lana Turner
75 minutes

RICH MAN, POOR GIRL

(*MGM, 1938*)
Director: Reinhold Schunzel
Producer: Edward Chodorov
Screenplay: Joseph A. Fields and Jerome Chodorov, based on the play "White Collars," by Edith Ellis
Photography: Ray June
Editor: Frank E. Hull
Cast: Robert Young, Lew Ayres, Ruth Hussey, Lana Turner, Rita Johnson
72 minutes

✳ ✳ ✳

DRAMATIC SCHOOL

(*MGM, 1938*)

Director: Robert B. Sinclair

Producer: Mervyn LeRoy

Screenplay: Ernst Vajd and Mary McCall, Jr., from the Hungarian play *School of Drama*, by Hans Szekely and Zolton Egyed

Photography: William Daniels

Editor: Frederick Y. Smith

Cast: Luise Rainer, Paulette Goddard, Alan Marshal, Lana Turner, Anthony Allen, Ann Rutherford, Hans Conried

80 minutes

CALLING DR. KILDARE

(*MGM, 1939*)

Director: Harold S. Bucquet

Producer: Lou Ostrow

Screenplay: Harry Ruskin and Willis Goldbeck, from an original story by Max Brand

Photography: Alfred Gilk and Lester White

Editor: Robert J. Kern

Cast: Lew Ayres, Lionel Barrymore, Laraine Day, Nat Pendleton, Lana Turner

86 minutes

DANCING CO-ED

(*MGM, 1939*)

Director: S. Sylvan Simon

Producer: Edgar Selwyn

Screenplay: Albert Mannheimer, based on a story by Albert Treynor

Photography: Alfred Gilks
Editor: W. Donn Hayes
Cast: Lana Turner, Richard Carlson, Artie Shaw, Ann Rutherford, Lee Bowman, Thurston Hall
84 minutes

TWO GIRLS ON BROADWAY
(MGM, 1940)
Director: S. Sylvan Simon
Producer: Jack Cummings
Screenplay: Joseph Fields and Jerome Chodorov, from a story by Edmund Goulding
Photography: George Folsey
Editor: Blanche Sewell
Cast: Lana Turner, Joan Blondell, George Murphy, Kent Taylor, Richard Lane
73 minutes

WE WHO ARE YOUNG
(MGM, 1940)
Director: Harold S. Bucquet
Producer: Seymour Nebenzahl
Screenplay: Dalton Trumbo, from an original story by Dalton Trumbo
Photography: Karl Freund
Editor: Howard O'Neill
Cast: Lana Turner, John Shelton, Gene Lockhart, Grant Mitchell, Jonathan Hale, Ian Wolfe
80 minutes

✳   ✳   ✳

ZIEGFELD GIRL

(MGM, 1941)

Director: Robert Z. Leonard

Producer: Pandro S. Berman

Screenplay: Marguerite Roberts and Sonya Levien, from an original story by William Anthony McQuire

Photography: Ray June

Editor: Blanche Sewell

Cast: James Stewart, Judy Garland, Hedy Lamarr, Lana Turner, Tony Martin, Jackie Cooper, Ian Hunter, Charles Winninger, Edward Everett Horton, Dan Dailey

131 minutes

DR. JEKYLL AND MR. HYDE

(MGM, 1941)

Producer and director: Victor Fleming

Screenplay: John Lee Mahin, based on the novel by Robert Louis Stevenson

Photography: Joseph Ruttenberg

Editor: Harold F. Kress

Cast: Spencer Tracy, Ingrid Bergman, Lana Turner, Donald Crisp, Ian Hunter

127 minutes

HONKY TONK

(MGM, 1941)

Director: Jack Conway

Producer: Pandro S. Berman

Screenplay: Marguerite Roberts and John Sanford

Photography: Harold Rosson

Editor: Blanche Sewell
Cast: Clark Gable, Lana Turner, Frank Morgan, Claire
    Trevor, Marjorie Main, Albert Dekker, Chill Wills
104 minutes

JOHNNY EAGER

(MGM, 1942)
Director: Mervyn LeRoy
Producer: John W. Considine
Screenplay: John Lee Mahin and James Edward Grant
Photography: Harold Rosson
Editor: Albert Akst
Cast: Robert Taylor, Lana Turner, Edward Arnold, Van
    Heflin, Robert Sterling, Patricia Dane
107 minutes

SOMEWHERE I'LL FIND YOU

(MGM, 1942)
Director: Wesley Ruggles
Producer: Pandro S. Berman
Screenplay: Marguerite Roberts, based on a story by
    Charles Hoffman and adapted by Walter Reisch
Photography: Harold Rosson
Editor: Frank E. Hull
Cast: Clark Gable, Lana Turner, Robert Sterling, Patricia
    Dane, Reginald Owen, Lee Patrick
108 minutes

✳   ✳   ✳

SLIGHTLY DANGEROUS
(*MGM, 1943*)
Director: Wesley Ruggles
Producer: Pandro S. Berman
Screenplay: Charles Lederer and George Oppenheimer, from a story by Ian McLellan Hunter and Aileen Hamilton
Photography: Harold Rosson
Editor: Frank E. Hull
Cast: Lana Turner, Robert Young, Walter Brennan, Dame May Whitty, Eugene Pallette, Alan Mowbray
94 minutes

THE YOUNGEST PROFESSION
(*MGM, 1943*)
Director: Edward Buzzell
Producer: B. F. Zeidman
Screenplay: George Oppenheimer, Charles Lederer, and Leonard Spigelgass, based on a book by Lillian Day
Photography: Charles Lawton
Editor: Ralph Winters
Cast: Virginia Weidler, Jean Porter, Edward Arnold, John Carroll
Cameo appearances by: Robert Taylor, Lana Turner, Greer Garson, Walter Pidgeon, William Powell
81 minutes

DUBARRY WAS A LADY
(*MGM, 1943*)
Director: Roy Del Ruth
Producer: Arthur Freed
Screenplay: Irving Brecher

Photography in Technicolor: Karl Freund
Editor: Blanche Sewell
Cast: Red Skelton, Lucille Ball, Gene Kelly; guest appearance by Lana Turner
101 minutes

MARRIAGE IS A PRIVATE AFFAIR

(MGM, 1944)
Director: Robert Z. Leonard
Producer: Pandro S. Berman
Screenplay: David Hertz and Lenore Coffee, based on a novel by Judith Kelly
Photography: Ray June
Editor: George White
Cast: Lana Turner, James Craig, John Hodiak, Frances Gifford
116 minutes

KEEP YOUR POWDER DRY

(MGM, 1945)
Director: Edward Buzzell
Producer: George Haight
Screenplay: Mary C. McCall, Jr., and George Bruce
Photography: Ray June
Editor: Frank E. Hull
Cast: Lana Turner, Laraine Day, Susan Peters, Agnes Moorehead
93 minutes

* * *

WEEKEND AT THE WALDORF
(MGM, 1945)
Director: Robert Z. Leonard
Producer: Arthur Hornblow, Jr.·
Screenplay: Sam and Bella Spewack, adapted by Guy Bolton from the novel and play *Grand Hotel,* by Vicki Baum
Photography: Robert Planck
Editor: Robert J. Kern
Cast: Ginger Rogers, Lana Turner, Walter Pidgeon, Van Johnson, Edward Arnold, Robert Benchley
130 minutes

THE POSTMAN ALWAYS RINGS TWICE
(MGM, 1946)
Director: Tay Garnett
Producer: Carey Wilson
Screenplay: Harry Ruskin and Niven Busch, based on the novel by James M. Cain
Photography: Sidney Wagner
Editor: George White
Cast: Lana Turner, John Garfield, Cecil Kellaway, Hume Cronyn, Leon Ames
113 minutes

GREEN DOLPHIN STREET
(MGM, 1947)
Director: Victor Saville
Producer: Carey Wilson
Screenplay: Samson Raphaelson, based on the novel by Elizabeth Goudge
Photography: George Folsey

Editor: George White

Cast: Lana Turner, Van Heflin, Donna Reed, Richard Hart, Frank Morgan, Linda Christian

141 minutes

CASS TIMBERLANE

(MGM, 1947)

Director: George Sidney

Producer: Arthur Hornblow, Jr.

Screenplay: Donald Ogden Stewart, based on the novel by Sinclair Lewis

Photography: Robert Planck

Editor: John Dunning

Cast: Spencer Tracy, Lana Turner, Zachary Scott, Tom Drake, Mary Astor, Albert Dekker

119 minutes

HOMECOMING

(MGM, 1948)

Director: Mervyn LeRoy

Producer: Sidney Franklin

Screenplay: Paul Osborn, based on an original story by Sidney Kingsley

Photography: Harold Rosson

Editor: John Dunning

Cast: Clark Gable, Lana Turner, Anne Baxter, John Hodiak

114 minutes

✳   ✳   ✳

THE THREE MUSKETEERS

(*MGM, 1948*)

Director: George Sidney

Producer: Pandro S. Berman

Screenplay: Robert Ardrey, from the novel by Alexandre Dumas

Photography: Robert Planck

Editors: Robert K. Kern and George Boemler

Cast: Lana Turner, Gene Kelly, June Allyson, Van Heflin, Angela Lansbury, Frank Morgan, Vincent Price

126 minutes

A LIFE OF HER OWN

(*MGM, 1950*)

Director: George Cukor

Producer: Voldemar Vetluguin

Screenplay: Isobel Lennart

Photography: George Folsey

Editor: George White

Gowns: Helen Rose

Makeup: William Tuttle

Cast: Lana Turner, Ray Milland, Tom Ewell, Louis Calhern, Barry Sullivan

108 minutes

MR. IMPERIUM

(*MGM, 1951*)

Director: Don Hartman

Producer: Edwin H. Knopf

Screenplay: Edwin H. Knopf and Don Hartman, from the play by Edwin H. Knopf

Photography: George J. Folsey

Editors: George White and William Gulick
Cast: Lana Turner, Ezio Pinza, Marjorie Main, Barry Sullivan, Sir Cedric Hardwicke
87 minutes

THE MERRY WIDOW
(MGM, 1952)
Director: Curtis Bernhardt
Producer: Joe Pasternak
Screenplay: Sonya Levien and William Ludwig, based on the operetta by Franz Lehar
Photography: Robert Surtees
Gowns: Helen Rose
Makeup: William Tuttle
Cast: Lana Turner, Fernando Lamas, Una Merkel
105 minutes

THE BAD AND THE BEAUTIFUL
(MGM, 1952)
Director: Vincente Minnelli
Producer: John Houseman
Screenplay: Charles Schnee, based on a story by George Bradshaw
Photography: Robert Surtees
Editor: Conrad A. Nervig
Cast: Lana Turner, Kirk Douglas, Walter Pidgeon, Dick Powell, Barry Sullivan, Gloria Grahame
117 minutes

✳ ✳ ✳

LATIN LOVERS

(*MGM, 1953*)

Director: Mervyn LeRoy

Producer: Joe Pasternak

Screenplay: Isobel Lennart

Photography: Joseph Ruttenberg

Editor: John McSweeney, Jr.

Cast: Lana Turner, Ricardo Montalban, John Lund, Jean Hagen

104 minutes

THE FLAME AND THE FLESH

(*MGM, 1954*)

Director: Richard Brooks

Producer: Joe Pasternak

Screenplay: Helen Deutsch, based on a novel by Auguste Bailly

Photography: Christopher Challis

Editors: Albert Akst and Ray Poulton

Cast: Lana Turner, Pier Angeli, Carlos Thompson

104 minutes

BETRAYED

(*MGM, 1954*)

Director and producer: Gottfried Reinhardt

Screenplay: Ronald Millar and George Froeschel

Photography: F. A. Young

Editors: John Dunning and Raymond Poulton

Cast: Clark Gable, Lana Turner, Victor Mature, Louis Calhern

111 minutes

✳   ✳   ✳

THE PRODIGAL

(*MGM, 1955*)

Director: Richard Thorpe
Producer: Charles Schnee
Screenplay: by Maurice Zimm, Joe Breen, Jr., and Samuel James Larsen, from the Bible story
Photography: Joseph Ruttenberg
Editor: Harold F. Kress
Cast: Lana Turner, Edmund Purdom, Louis Calhern, Audrey Dalton, James Mitchell

115 minutes

THE SEA CHASE

(*Warner Bros., 1955*)

Producer and director: John Farrow
Screenplay: James Warner Bellah and John Twist, from the novel by Andrew Geer
Photography: William Clothier
Editor: William Ziegler
Cast: John Wayne, Lana Turner, David Farrar, Tab Hunter

117 minutes

THE RAINS OF RANCHIPUR

(*20th Century-Fox, 1955*)

Director: Jean Negulesco
Producer: Frank Ross
Screenplay: Merle Miller, based on the novel *The Rains Came*, by Louis Bromfield
Photography: Milton Krasner
Editor: Dorothy Spencer

Cast: Lana Turner, Richard Burton, Fred MacMurray, Joan Caulfield, Michael Rennie
104 minutes

DIANE

(MGM, 1956)
Director: David Miller
Producer: Edwin H. Knopf
Screenplay: Christopher Isherwood, based on the story by John Erskine
Photography: Robert Planck
Editor: John McSweeney
Cast: Lana Turner, Pedro Armendariz, Roger Moore, Marisa Pavan, Sir Cedric Hardwicke
110 minutes

PEYTON PLACE

(A Jerry Wald Production for 20th Century-Fox, 1957)
Director: Mark Robson
Producer: Jerry Wald
Screenplay: John Michael Hayes from the novel by Grace Metalious
Photography: William Mellor
Editor: David Bretherton
Cast: Lana Turner, Hope Lange, Lee Philips, Lloyd Nolan, Diane Varsi, Arthur Kennedy, Russ Tamblyn, Terry Moore
157 minutes

✳   ✳   ✳

THE LADY TAKES A FLYER
(*Universal-International, 1958*)
Director: Jack Arnold
Producer: William Alland
Screenplay: Danny Arnold, from a story by Edmund H. North
Photography: Irving Glassberg
Editor: Sherman Todd
Cast: Lana Turner, Jeff Chandler, Richard Denning, Chuck Conners
93 minutes

ANOTHER TIME, ANOTHER PLACE
(*A Lanturn Production for Paramount Release, 1958*)
Director: Lewis Allen
Producer: Joseph Kaufman
Assistant Producer: Del Armstrong
Screenplay: Stanley Mann, based on a novel by Lenore Coffee
Photography: Jack Hildyard
Editor: Geoffrey Foot
Cast: Lana Turner, Barry Sullivan, Glynis Johns, Sean Connery
98 minutes

IMITATION OF LIFE
(*Universal-International, 1959*)
Director: Douglas Sirk
Producer: Ross Hunter
Screenplay: Eleanore Griffin and Allan Scott, based on the novel by Fannie Hurst
Photography: Russell Metty

Editor: Milton Carruth
Cast: Lana Turner, John Gavin, Sandra Dee, Dan O'Her-
    lihy, Robert Alda, Juanita Moore, Troy Donahue
125 minutes

PORTRAIT IN BLACK

(Universal-International, 1960)
Director: Michael Gordon
Producer: Ross Hunter
Screenplay: Ivan Goff and Ben Roberts, based on their play
Photography: Russell Metty
Editor: Milton Carruth
Cast: Lana Turner, Anthony Quinn, Sandra Dee, John
    Saxon, Richard Basehart, Lloyd Nolan
112 minutes

BY LOVE POSSESSED

(Mirisch Pictures with Seven Arts for United Artists,
1961)
Director: John Sturges
Producer: Walter Mirisch
Screenplay: John Dennis, based on the novel by James
    Gould Cozzens
Photography: Russell Metty
Editor: Ferris Webster
Cast: Lana Turner, Efrem Zimbalist, Jr., Jason Robards,
    Jr., George Hamilton, Barbara Bel Geddes, Thomas
    Mitchell
115 minutes

* * *

BACHELOR IN PARADISE

(Ted Richmond Production released by MGM, 1961)

Director: Jack Arnold

Producer: Ted Richmond

Screenplay: Valentine Davis and Hal Kanter, based on the novel by Vera Caspary

Photography: Joseph Ruttenberg

Editor: Richard W. Farrell

Cast: Bob Hope, Lana Turner, Janis Paige, Jim Hutton, Paula Prentiss, Don Porter, Agnes Moorehead

108 minutes

WHO'S GOT THE ACTION?

(Amro-Claude-Mea Production for Paramount Pictures, 1962)

Director: Daniel Mann

Producer: Jack Rose

Screenplay: Jack Rose, based on the novel *Four Horseplayers Are Missing*, by Alexander Rose

Photography: Joseph Ruttenberg

Editor: Howard Smith

Cast: Dean Martin, Lana Turner, Eddie Albert, Nita Talbot, Walter Matthau, Paul Ford

93 minutes

LOVE HAS MANY FACES

(A Jerry Bresler Production for Columbia Pictures Release, 1965)

Director: Alexander Singer

Producer: Jerry Bresler

Screenplay: Marguerite Roberts

Photography: Joseph Ruttenberg

Editor: Alma Macrorie
Wardrobe for Miss Turner: Edith Head
Cast: Lana Turner, Cliff Robertson, Hugh O'Brian, Ruth Roman, Stephanie Powers
105 minutes

MADAME X

(A Ross Hunter Production for Universal Pictures, 1966)
Director: David Lowell Rich
Producer: Ross Hunter
Screenplay: Jean Holloway, based on the play by Alexandre Bisson
Photography: Russell Metty
Editor: Milton Carruth
Cast: Lana Turner, John Forsythe, Ricardo Montalban, Burgess Meredith, Constance Bennett
100 minutes

THE BIG CUBE

(A Warner Bros.-Seven Arts Release of a Francisco Diez Barroso Production, 1969)
Director: Tito Davison
Producer: Lindsley Parsons
Screenplay: William Douglas Lansford, from a story by Tito Davison and Edmundo Baez
Photography: Gabriel Figueroa
Editor: Carlos Savage, Jr.
Cast: Lana Turner, George Chakiris, Richard Egan
98 minutes

✳ ✳ ✳

PERSECUTION

(A *Tyburn Film Production, 1974*)
Director: Don Chaffey
Producer: Kevin Francis
Screenplay: Robert B. Hutton and Rosemary Wooten,
    based on their original story
Photography: Kenneth Talbot
Editor: Mike Campbell
Cast: Lana Turner, Trevor Howard, Ralph Bates
88 minutes

BITTERSWEET LOVE

(*Avco Embassy Pictures, 1976*)
Director: David Miller
Producer: Zappala-Slott
Screenplay: Adrian Morrall and D. A. Kellogg
Cast: Lana Turner, Robert Alda, Celeste Holm, Robert
    Lansing, Meredith Baxter-Birney

✳ SELECTED BIBLIOGRAPHY ✳

Arce, Hector. *The Secret Life of Tyrone Power.* New York: William Morrow and Company, 1979.

Crane, Cheryl. *Detour.* New York: Arbor House/William Morrow and Company, 1988.

Douglas, Kirk. *The Ragman's Son.* New York: Simon and Schuster, 1988.

Guiles, Fred Lawrence. *Tyrone Power: The Last Idol.* New York: Doubleday, 1979.

Graham, Sheilah. *Hollywood Revisited.* New York: St. Martin's Press, 1984.

Harris, Warren G. *Gable and Lombard.* New York: Simon and Schuster, 1974.

LeRoy, Mervyn. *Take One.* New York: Hawthorne Books, 1974.

Morella, Joe, and Edward Z. Epstein. *Lana: The Public and Private Lives of Miss Turner.* New York: Citadel Press, 1971.

Parish, James Robert, and Ronald L. Bowers. *The MGM Stock Company.* New York: Arlington House, 1974.

Pero, Taylor, and Jeff Rovin. *Always Lana.* New York: Bantam Books, Inc., 1982.

Rooney, Mickey. *Life Is Too Short*. New York: Villard Books, 1991.

Shepherd Donald, and Robert Slatzer. *Duke: The Life and Times of John Wayne*. New York: Zebra Books, 1985.

Shipman, David. *The Great Movie Stars: The Golden Years*. New York: Crown, 1970.

Thomas, Bob. *Joan Crawford*. New York: Simon and Schuster, 1978.

Turner, Lana. *Lana: The Lady, the Legend, the Truth*. New York: Dutton, 1982.

Valentino, Lou. *The Films of Lana Turner*. New York: Citadel Press, 1976.

Wayne, Jane Ellen. *Robert Taylor: The Man with the Perfect Face*. New York: St. Martin's Press, 1987.

———. *Clark Gable: Portrait of a Misfit*. New York: St. Martin's Press, 1993.

✳ INDEX ✳